SELECTED POEMS

ROBERT DUNCAN
SELECTED POEMS

REVISED AND ENLARGED

Edited by Robert J. Bertholf

A NEW DIRECTIONS BOOK

Portions of this book appear by arrangement with The University of California Press.

Manufactured in the United States of America
New Directions Books are printed on acid-free paper.
This revised and enlarged edition first published as New Directions Paperbook 838 in 1997
Published simultaneously in Canada by Penguin Books Canada Limited

Library of Congress Cataloging in Publication Data

Duncan, Robert Edward, 1919–
    [Poems. Selections]
    Selected poems / Robert Duncan; edited by Robert J. Bertholf. —
Rev. and enl.
        p.   cm. — (New Directions paperbook ; 838)
    Includes index.
    ISBN 0–8112–1345–5 (acid-free paper)
    I. Bertholf, Robert J.   II. Title.
PS3507.U629A6   1997
811'.54—dc20   96–43881
                                                       CIP

SECOND PRINTING

New Directions Books are published for James Laughlin
by New Directions Publishing Corporation,
80 Eighth Avenue, New York 10011

Contents

Introduction

"The imagination of the cosmos," Robert Duncan wrote in his essay "Towards an Open Universe," is as immediate to me as the imagination of my household or my self." Duncan's poetry is filled with common details of living as well as fanciful discoveries; statements of the daily enterprise as well as prophecies of world order. Myths, stories from various countries, the lore of nations, and the visions of art come into these poems. He is a poet of profound learning and perpetual innocence.

Robert Duncan was born in Oakland, California, January 7, 1919. His mother died in childbirth; he was adopted and spent his early years in Oakland and Bakersfield, California. In 1936, he enrolled at the University of California at Berkeley. Even at this period, his commitment to poetry was serious and determined. During the late 1930s and early 1940s, he read and became devoted to the work of Ezra Pound, D.H. Lawrence, Edith Sitwell, Laura Riding, James Joyce, Gertrude Stein, and H.D. He derived his poetry and poetics from the great masters of modernist writing, as well as from Dante, Shakespeare, Blake, Emerson, and Thomas Carlyle. He spent periods of time in New York City, where he was part of the group of artists living and working around Anaïs Nin. He knew Roberto Matta and Hans Hofmann, and so witnessed the emergence of an American version of Surrealism, centered for a time in *View*, a magazine of art and poetry in which he published one poem in 1942. He followed the emergence of "Abstract Expressionism" in the museums and galleries, as well as the developments of modernism in exhibitions of Bonnard, Villard, Matisse, and Picasso. By 1946, he was back in Berkeley. This was the beginning of a dynamic period for poetry in the Bay Area. Jack Spicer and Robin Blaser became friends, and together they devised "serial form" for a series of poems linked by repeating themes. Duncan, Blaser, and many others attended the literary and anarchist meetings of Kenneth Rexroth, whose wisdom and range of interests influenced emerging poets who soon after commanded national attention in a movement called the "San Francisco Renaissance" in poetry. Though he was in Mallorca writing the poems for *Caesar's Gate, Letters*, and first poems for *The Opening of the Field* when Allen Ginsberg read "Howl" at the Six Gallery, October 13, 1955, Duncan was a major force in the articulation of a "New American Poetry" during the 1950s and 1960s in San Francisco. He was not part of "The Beat Movement," but he was one of a group of San Francisco poets and painters whose work changed the direction of literary and artistic history in America.

In 1947, Duncan met Charles Olson, but their discussions in Berkeley were about the Western migrations and the place of the city in history, not about a new poetry. Their literary association did not develop until the 1950s. By then, Olson had introduced Duncan to the work of Robert Creeley; Denise Levertov joined Duncan's literary community soon after. *The Black Mountain Review* and *Origin* were then key journals where Duncan, Olson, Creeley, Levertov, Paul Blackburn, Ed Dorn, Joel Oppenheimer, and others published the poems that became known as "Black Mountain Poetry." Duncan was surrounded by artists and poets wherever he was; the community of poets around Olson, Creeley, Levertov and Helen Adam provoked the writing and publication of Duncan's books *The Opening of the Field, Roots and Branches*, and *Bending the Bow*. Yet the various poetics of the poets associated with Olson, as well as those from the "San Francisco Renaissance," did not fully contain Duncan's ideas of his poems as a "grand collage"—a collection and formation of visual and textual images from a vast diversity of sources within a new contextual complexity. The painter Jess was his life companion from 1951 until Duncan's death in February 1988. Jess's work in collage and composition on canvas stimulated the visual details of language which informed Duncan's poetry. In his final two books, *Ground Work: Before The War* and *Ground Work: In the Dark*, Duncan releases the full power of his visual and verbal power. The elegiac complaint of the early poems appears in the late poems as a grim prophecy of humanity's course. Duncan published 40 books and pamphlets (plus broadsides and small publications), including a book of collected essays, *Fictive Certainties*. Chapters of an extended study of H.D., called "The H.D. Book," appeared in magazines beginning in the early 1960s, but he did not finish writing the book itself.

The poems in this volume (including the ones added for this second, enlarged edition) have been selected from the whole course of Duncan's work as primary examples of his attentions as a poet. He was intensely aware of his role as a poet, mindful too of his responsibilities. Meditations on the activity of poetry come in as frequently as discussions of the form of poetry, as in "Poetry Disarranged," the series "The Structure of Rime," and "Everything Speaks to Me." He wrote in many forms—songs, meditations, sonnets, prose poems (like the imitations of Gertrude Stein in *Writing Writing*), and a variety of stanzas, those in "The Ballad of the

Enamord Mage," for example. Early poems, like "Among My Friends Love Is a Great Sorrow," introduce the lyric mode in Duncan's poetry, which comes back again in "The Horns of Artemis," "Often I Am Permitted To Return To A Meadow," "Achilles' Song," and "The Sentinels." He was also interested in the sources of the poem in ancient myth, and all sorts of ancient wisdom and contemporary versions. From the early *Medieval Scenes* to "Before the Judgment, Passages 35" and "In Blood's Domaine [Passages]," Duncan sought out rhymes and connections with what Ezra Pound called the "deposit" of literature, but made the poem fully contemporary in his arrangement. *Medieval Scenes* also introduces "serial form" into Duncan's work. Based in part on Saturday afternoon movie episodes of the Lone Ranger and Tom Mix, the "serial poem" presents a series of poems that are related while each poem is also complete within itself. The "serial form" provides the structure for the later series, "The Structure of Rime" and "The Passages Poems," which Duncan wrote over a thirty-year period. The other major long poem of the early period, which is not included in this selection, is "The Venice Poem." This poem, compacted with very personal and very complex historical references, is based on "symphonic form," a kind of organization that Duncan did not use repeatedly in his later work.

Duncan's early poems are elegiac. They long for love and lament the failure to find it, as well as the pain of not realizing, at once, ideal aspirations. Yet the elegiac mode leads to the meditations on love in poems like "The Song of the Borderguard," "My Mother Would Be A Falconress," "The Torso, Passages 18," and "Circulations of the Song." Love is as essential for maintaining a domestic household ("The Household") as it is for entering the mythological household of mankind. The love of mankind, for mankind, as Dante says, should lead to benefits "for the good of the people," but in Duncan's view, politics, political systems, wars, and corruption twist and defeat human aspiration, and the desire for life filled with imaginative actuality. In many poems, "A Poem Beginning With a Line By Pindar," or "Before the Judgment, Passages 35," for examples, Duncan's elegiac voice becomes a prophetic voice of great perception. He insisted on the value of the poem, the force of love in the human community, and revelation of mythological presences in everyday events. In his view, each poem achieved its own specific form. Each poem is an enactment of a mind conceiving thought in language.

A Note on the Texts. When Duncan reprinted his poems in the collections *Selected Poems* (1959), *The Years as Catches* (1966), *The First Decade: Selected Poems 1940–1950* (1968), and *Derivations: Selected Poems 1950–*

1956 (1968), he made revisions in spacing, stanzas breaks, line breaks, spelling, and punctuation, and, to a lesser extent, he rewrote lines or groups of lines. A common revision was the change of the final d to t, as in "passd" changed to "passt." I have taken into account those revisions, the ones Duncan made after publication, as well as common spelling and typographical errors that entered the texts. My intention is to present a clean text for reading.

Robert J. Bertholf
The Poetry Collection
The State University of New York at Buffalo
May 1996

SELECTED POEMS

PERSEPHONE

"We have passed the great Trauma.
These wounds disclose our loss."

memory: farfields of morning,
       maimd winter, wheel and hoofhammerd weeds,
bare patches of earth. We heard rumor of the rape
among the women who wait at the wells with dry urns,
talk among leaves and among the old men
who sift tin cans and seashells searching for driftwood
to make fires on cold hearthstones. Stone hearts
and arteries hardend to stone.
                This sound of our mourning, wailing of reeds,
comes over the ice and the grey wastes of water.
We listen: it shrieks thru the ruins of cities,
whistles in shellholes
and freezes like ether in our lungs.

Shades falling under the oakshadow . . . shade upon shade
intent with their sorrow. The lust of such sorrow
listless, moving over the leafmold,
footmolded and hoofmolded, spoors of past violence.
From such clay our roots writhe, sucking the life
from corpsemold and footclay
and mold of the skull rooting.

Spore-spotted Onan, baldheaded, trickling with seed,
moved among us, or troops of swift women pursuing the leopard
passd. The quiet unbroken, dark beneath dark
branches spotted with light; or a flute in the morning
made truce, awakening the leaves like birds.
We shot green from the bark to flute music,
moving out from the trunk in a dream.

1

The sun was like gold on my body,
roots in the cold dark below me and arms
from the slender trunk showerd in gold light and shadows,
fingers green seeking the sun.

Lost, lost such peace, and Persephone lost.
Last dream brought silence,
silent thread of death-threatening dream.

We remember in symbols such violence:
the splintering of rock, the shock of the trauma,
in which she was taken from us. Shade
falls under the shadow . . . shade upon shade.
Spotted with bonewhite, splinter of driftwood,
the bark wet with terror, no sleep,
only waiting. Only we wait, our wounds barely heald
for the counterattack before sunrise.

PASSAGE OVER WATER

We have gone out in boats upon the sea at night,
lost, and the vast waters close traps of fear about us.
The boats are driven apart, and we are alone at last
under the incalculable sky, listless, diseased with stars.

Let the oars be idle, my love, and forget at this time
our love like a knife between us
defining the boundaries that we can never cross
nor destroy as we drift into the heart of our dream,
cutting the silence, slyly, the bitter rain in our mouths
and the dark wound closed in behind us.

Forget depth-bombs, death and promises we made,
gardens laid waste, and, over the wastelands westward,
the rooms where we had come together bombd.

But even as we leave, your love turns back. I feel
your absence like the ringing of bells silenced. And salt
over your eyes and the scales of salt between us. Now,

you pass with ease into the destructive world.
There is a dry crash of cement. The light fails,
falls into the ruins of cities upon the distant shore
and within the indestructible night I am alone.

THE YEARS AS CATCHES

This century, an iron bell of joy, has scarcely rung
its first harsh notes of morning, scarcely rung
upon our ears the strident ecstasy in God. The bloody dawn
is scarcely with us. In the unpierc'd sky
it gathers. In the unsounded August, cold & early sight
bestirs my soul. Is this a later hour then, when Milton, he
past twenty-three, saw that year
gone from him, stood in the hasting days of his soul's April,
stood in the weary stretch of Christendom
impatient for the green, the bud & bloom
of manhood? Is this a later hour when we rise? For I
have lost already more than youth & all brief timely joy.

Already ere I wake I hear that makes disturbing
all this dear & pleasant world about me so devised
in harmonie where we would, fallen, see
in gardens chaos—I hear the clamor of that bell
ring rathe upon my ears like iron. I hunger
for that testing that would sound the deep of grace,
that pure & metal spirit ring upon my soul at last
in which twas forged. Already ere I wake
I hear that sound. Shout & fill the air with sirens.
No sound that you can make for war or human misery
can meet that sound nor cover it. No waste you wrake
upon the body, no ravaging of mind nor spirit can
make deaf nor blind nor insensate. No pounding, strife,
no battles, nor repentance nor moaning over dead,
shall divert this sound once known. A single note
across the human image, endlessly repeated, so
that all that maimd, incapable and clouded metal
will be pain, all that insensate & battling structure
hungry upon itself that first deliberated blindness shall

be brought to sight, the mute unanswering rock of self
cry out. Nor be there refuge. Virtue,
charity and hope avail not. This century
has scarcely rung its brightness nor laid bare
that clear unbearable sound world against whose purity
we set store a little blindness, we would make
an interim eternity, momentous war & peace, estate
and settlement, lament or celebrate a youth or age
that yet shall not avail against the still
unbroken universe of God.

*

But O the heavy change, now thou art gone,
now thou art gone, and we are set adrift in th'eclipse.

Any wastes, like Carthage burnd & salted,
cities of despair, are better in the mind
than beauty, more coveted. Shall we
be less in sin than Adam to repeat like canker
in the rose of self our greed for counterfeit delight,
that pass our word upon the scene, time's slaves,
bewail the autumn harshly come
ere there has been a month of green? Shall we
claim virtue, love of freedom, who've confined
our spirit, each his own, who've set
the worm to feed upon our conscience, nor turn
from leisure and these ill-gaind days
but that would make our peace
with no peace in us, keep
a brutish silence in adversity.

I brood upon these lines of Milton, words
where there moves such a tide to feed
my restlessness. Where shall we sometime meet
in this dark land no longer having
darkness in us? And bring our tired souls home
to linger over wine about a fire, to hear
with equal grace a little Mozart playd
within the gloom of an Autumnal room, to linger

over these last rude & somber moments
come to rest.

*

Lift, untimely joy.
Impatiently I
to break the day, unending bread
of morning light, waked
into scarce time to make
my peace with April, with the rose
that bled
life from my bloody heart
unsounded cold of love,
an ecstasy, all year as of
all youth to never cease,
to part
with no immediate grace,
continual
earliness to no fulfillment, lift
thy face,
His harmony, my Chaos.

The never flies, the impatient joy,
in whose untime repeated I
in the hasting days, His still
His clamorous bright day, see still
that unbroken rose that broken is
no other cross than love.

Break in the ear the sounding sight
of Mozart. Break this manhood, harsh
& misery, lift the light
into the throat until
the broken cross, the body-rose
will close,
my Harmony, His chaos.

O lift into
that singleness,

no earliness. As free
as sight from eye,
as sound from ear,
as Truth from Lie,
His ecstasy ring forth from me,
from what was misery,
as from the darkness of the night
ring forth this light.

Catch from the years the line of joy,
impatient & repeated day,
my heart, break. Eye
break open and set free
His world, my ecstasy.

HOMAGE AND LAMENT FOR EZRA POUND
IN CAPTIVITY MAY 12, 1944

Apprehension this spring . . . the leaves, the leaves,
still, as still as everness returnd,
defining distances with green. The space between
alive with each upon each barely in motion.
Coming into a room from hidden windows, light
reflects in shade a spotted shade of spring
having almost sound upon the ear. Four voices
—violin, viola, cello and bass, appear and reappear
upon a warp and woof of distances
unified in light and sense of leaves, of Venus
sea-ambulant among the boughs. The numerous leaves
are still, as still as the heart in seeing, in hearing
—a melody within an edifice of sound, as sound
as Brzeska's head in solid stone made, as lasting
in the heart though the particular stone be crackt.
Iconoclasts may never break that stone once seen,
once heard in the returning everness of mind.
The numerous leaves are still in seeing, in hearing.
The numerous leaves await in knowing
apprehension this spring like some crackt voice
fanatic dryad among the boughs, the melodies
of mind.

                    Ezra, this time of year,
this deceptive real we fear lest hunting voices
overtake the hunted. Torn by wild upon the wild
evasive beauty, a mocking face recalls to mind
among the leaves, the lights, an enemy.
Far down—I hang in qualms of deep—
an old man stumbles,
mutters maledictions upon the hounds.

In this place, before Hell's door, anger-blind,
leaves rehearse crimes. Human figures in a frieze
rehearse rememberd faces. Universities, the damnd,
seas of human faces go down like wolves
behind the eyes to fill these distances with fire.
The desire, for all its leaves, for all of violin,
of solid stone, turns a human hurt and damnd
toward outrage's Hell. Desire has crackt
crosst eyes to see a Hell's door Heaven.
Hell's door's Heaven will never change as leaves
may change and fall like wolves
upon the human flesh and bone. Universities,
the damnd, that turn upon the damnd
with passive righteousness—another hell,
more treacherous than fire or wolves.
Far down—I voice in the wrong beauty
better than no beauty—to see a still world still
hopping mad among its calm of leaves.

                *

We have not less to fear or hate. Old man, early
devoted voice, this afternoon as light falls down
it leaves one shining sill, promising, illusive.
The room is filld, enters in the mind, with this,
an architecture to house the mind in Heaven—
apprehending in a single phrase of Mozart
a universe, the tones, the tones like leaves of light
to fall, to reappear, establishing distances
upon the warp and woof of person not to fall.
A single window upon another scene,
upon a painted Mediterranean blueness in the room,

gives possession of a world by love.
Against some Mediterranean scene an old man
stumbles, mutters maledictions, sees that blue,
as Joyce once saw a sea, tighten scrotum,
mock at an old man's heart.

He screams abominations, curses, seeing a gull
fly up upon the wind, seeing an early eagerness
falter and drift to be toucht by usury.
What still and wondrous knowledge
avails then? to know as leaves, as sea of soul
gives out, no longer capable to eager green,
to see each upon each barely in motion
as still as everness returnd. Apprehension this spring
. . . the leaves, the leaves,
still, as still as everness returning.

"AMONG MY FRIENDS LOVE IS A GREAT SORROW"

Among my friends love is a great sorrow.
It has become a daily burden, a feast,
a gluttony for fools, a heart's famine.
We visit one another asking, telling one another.
We do not burn hotly, we question the fire.
We do not fall forward with our alive
eager faces looking thru into the fire.
We stare back into our own faces.
We have become our own realities.
We seek to exhaust our lovelessness.

Among my friends love is a painful question.
We seek out among the passing faces
a sphinx-face who will ask its riddle.
Among my friends love is an answer to a question
that has not been askt.
Then ask it.

Among my friends love is a payment.
It is an old debt for a borrowing foolishly spent.

And we go on, borrowing and borrowing
         from each other.

Among my friends love is a wage
that one might have for an honest living.

I AM A MOST FLESHLY MAN

I am a most fleshly man, and see
in your body what stirs my spirit.
And my spirit is intimate of my hand,
intimate of my breast and heart,
intimate of my parted lips
that would seek their solace
in your lips.

Receive me; worn and warm body I am.
I am a most fleshly fire, and yearn
for your body to replenish my flame.
I would embrace you and name myself
anew in your flesh.

The green of eucalyptus boughs
hung in the distances of the air.
Les terraces au clair de la lune
playd in the orb of the afternoon, blue
and sunlit area where
we moved.
The *japonaiserie* of bay
and islands in the smoky haze
seemd to bear the fine imprint,
distinct and lonely, of the mind's design,
and beckoning intimation of a love
in which the days like swallows flew,
one by one, from the heart's dim grove
to trace in their flight the lineaments of truth.
I spoke to you and tried to say
I seek the body's rest in grace.

O I should have knelt upon the floor
and wept.
I should have surrenderd to the body's faith
and knelt,
suppliant to the hour's god that came
and went,
a luminous shadow in the blood.

I have made my vow in flesh, and see
in you the body's golden covenant.
And the spirit is intimate of your hand,
intimate of your breast and lips.
I woo that carnal sacrament of you,
the lover's testament of faith
in which in body we release
the spirit's immortality.

Come unto me, questioning dark spirit.
You dwell upon the threshold of my mind.
This yearning is a vast eternity
that waste about us questioning lies,
and we, in the limbo of disembodied love,
stare upon the bodies we deny.

I am a most fleshly fire.
I would embrace you in that flame,
and we should lie brought then to rest
and gaze, gaze upon each other in that hour
when newly created each in the other
we hang like smoky music in the air.

Medieval Scenes [1950]

*Upon the wall of her bed chamber, so the legend
goes, the poetess Laura Riding had inscribed in
letters of gold:* GOD IS A WOMAN

THE DREAMERS

The genius mixt too strong a cup.
At noon the lethargy remains.
We cannot shake it off.

Sleep lingers all our lifetime in our eyes
as night at midday hovers
in the fir tree boughs.
The Genius brews his lethal cup.
All things swim and glitter.

The magic in convolutions of our company
winks its lights. Its touch is slight
and vital. But we are bearish magickers,
makers of lightnings in half-sleep of furry storm.

It is the magic of not-touching,
not-looking sharpenings of the eye,
dim thunders of imaginings. Half-loves
kept short of love's redeeming fire,

temperd to fear and sharpend
to a knife-edge cut. It flashes
in the air. But we are bear-like
dreamers in a lifetime's hibernation,

the sleep of summer's heroes,
of romance's mountain magic. The shadow hovers
in the doom bejeweld fir and whispers.
The daemon swims and glitters in each face.

11

Each sleepy bearish hero short of love
recounts his dreams. The fir
casts on the day's continuum of light
a shade of language dragon red with hope.

It is the magic of not-touching,
the hostile speech of rigid magickers.
And we are unawakend dreamers,
sleep-talking miseries of animal despair.

I have within my heart a tree, a fir
of shadows, Hibernia of dreams.
"The Speech," I said, "is sexual.
It tells our lovers what we are; excites
the hesitating ear of an animal mind."

"But beasts," then Curran said, "at least
would nudge each other."

THE HELMET OF GOLIATH

What if the poet in a moment of terror
or memory of a terrible event
is not like David, but David himself?

This is the Helmet of Goliath.

"Goliath stopt," the poet writes—
"he heard his armor creak
"and grew alive with its increasing weight
"and felt a cooling night creep on the land."

Is it mere song, or memory?

The windy armor grows alive with song
and in that darkend helmet
the poet's face is curious. The lonely men
about the revolutionary table sit.
They seem to muse, each man so solitary,

or, like excited Oracles in conversations after hours,
speak secrets of their trade.

The helmet sings:

Cry woe upon the sleeping land.
A revolution works unknowing there.
The lonely knight in Goliath's poetry of armor
is not Goliath. He was a spirit of power,
fallen away into a dark disuse.
See how the beauty of his form
has been deformd! He wears
a doom bejeweld bright of armory.

Cry woe upon the sleeping land.
It grows alive with an increasing weight.
There is a secret wooing in the night,
a fine adultery of voices talking.
I saw the sleight-of-look, the moment's
quick avowals. It vanisht,
wraith-like elegance
of a forbidden swan.

The solitary muse
speaks to each man. They grieve
and shake their heads. They grieve
that grief can teach them nothing
nor can they touching touch.

The poets at their table speak of love.
The waves of an uncomprehending sea
wash between each lover and his love.
The words are drownd of meaning in that roar.

Goliath from a distance fell
into a dark of meaning.

The roar within the helmet makes us deaf.
It grows alive. We never seem to reach our life.

The sword, our innerness,
is sleight-of-soul, it vanishes.

The speech of the poets seems to deny
all love. They listen to forbidden music.
And in that darkend helmet
each poet's face is curious.

THE BANNERS

The Swan is the signet, heraldic joy.
The Banners make animate the inanimate day.
No longer mere, but night-mare changed.
The Swan, the sign, displays its grace.

The lion in the loin that slumbers
shakes the sheath of sleep back from his claws
and stretches. The poets
weave upon that tapestry a spell
of flowering, gold-threaded tendrils of a vine;
make animate each animal form
with conceit of loving. There

as if washt up upon a wave of violet,
of blue, vermillion and clear yellow,
the poets animate a unicorn,
animalization of the beckoning swan.
This is the night-mare thread of their loom.

The days before awakenings, dark ages,
are long with hours for the poet's tapestry.
The unicorn of gold and swan-white threads
nuzzles the sleeping virgin in the park.
Above their heads the signet of the Prince
is woven, elaborate blood-red signature.

The poets weave themselves as the erotic hunters.
They wear bright jerkins of a rich brocade
and silk of forest green upon their thighs.

They stand with instruments of hunting,
hooded falcons, spears and nets,
and watch that sleeping nakedness
where they had woven her,
half-hidden in the flowery spread upon the ground.
They smile mysteriously upon their innocence
and upon their unicorn, virgin wildness brought to bay.
Swan into unicorn, innocence to wildness,
brought to bay.

They seem unconscious of the signature.
It glimmers in embroidery of leaves,
the scarlet lake of some significance.

THE KINGDOM OF JERUSALEM

The hosts of the glittering fay return.
Their sunken palaces in lakes of dream
rise, amaze, and perish.

What of avowals then, fealties of ruin?
The splendid Emperor of Jerusalem dreams
of the Emperor of Jerusalem in his splendor.
The poets at their board
subvert the empire with their sorrow.
Powerless and melancholy, the young men smile
evasively and stroll
along the shores of the slumbering lake. We hear
the diapasons of a drownd magnificence.

Then, then the agony came.
"There is something else," I said.
I had not known
I had so deep a sorrowing.

The knights are luminous with the dreamer's splendor.
I serve the unease of an early promise.
I remember now the sea was calm,
the wind had fallen into a still of potency.

The sails hung slack, and the Sun in His heavens
was the Lion of our sorrow. I drank
the draft from a secret thirst.

The people of the goddess Danu smile
evasively and work their spell.

The poets are foolish in their wise.
They stroll like gallants in the park of days,
attended by their shadows that are hounds
of a disturbing wonder.

O but these gallants seem so calm,
they fall into a still of potency,
listless, uneasy rememberers.

The palaces of the fay appear.
We seem to hear the battle cry, or love cry,
or death cry,   the last haloo
of some deserted lover's horn,   lost
upon a field we had forgotten,   amaze
and perish.

THE FESTIVALS

Was it a dream, or was it memory?
"I do not want the witless rounds of spring
to break this fine enchantment.
The joy unbroken is the lovely thing."

The poet sees his foolish Muse bestir herself
as if to shake off foolishness. "The sleeping joy,"
he murmurs in her dream, "is best.

"Then let us drift upon the fire with closed eyes,
pretend our midnight. When we dead awaken
we will find our ecstasy
will break into the maddest of all noons.

"I would avoid the chattering of birds,
the twittering in gid and gawdy wide awake.
Our unicorn is but a gilded ass
adornd by village fools with a single horn
of painted wood.

"Faces too bright, janglings of love too live,
in the candid minds of the redeemd
these do not appear. I do not want
the wantonness of spring
to break my wonder into a spiritless chuckle,
piebald ribaldry of nights and days."

The poet holds the musing body that he loves,
and, like that glistening lover that Saint Julian knew,
that body has a leprous questioning of his soul.
All lovers, male and female hungers, move
in transformations of the Muse.
The Muse is wide awake.

"The joy awake," she says,
"is everywhere. You are a wondrous sleeping
in a world of wonders. The braying ass
the fools have painted gold and red
and decorated with a single horn
—I saw him in my dream and dreamt
he was a magic wonder. Now awake
I see he is a braying foolish unicorn."

The Muse, amused,
awakens the fearful poet to her dream.

THE MIRROR

Two women stroll among the orange-trees.
Reflected in the glass their nakedness
is like a feud of brilliancies.
One woman's hair is of a lewd gold,
red as man's first thought of sin.

It falls across the heavy indolence of her thighs
and barely sweeps the ground with gold.

The second woman has grown old.
Her naked body sags and wrinkles in its lust.
It speaks cavernous wastages of a despair.
She grins and shows her broken teeth.
The glass is like a rose of broken teeth.
It trembles with the waverings of the air.

The mirror does not ask if they are witches.
It watches. There is a naked man
between them. He twists between his thumb and finger
one nipple of the woman with the hair of gold.

She stands like an unknowing Eve,
radiant with evil, and waits. He holds
the nipple like a blood-red cherry there
between his curious extended fingers.

The daughters of Danaus lead their naked husbands,
each her naked husband to the naked bed.
There is a carnal burning in the air.

The woman with the fiery hair plays on a lute
the plaint of some erotic melody.
"I have within my heart of hearts a tree,"
she sings, *"that bears no fruit but misery."*

The man is standing with one foot
placed forward. He holds
the aged witch's dugs with his two hands
and thrusts his blood red penis in the air.

She touches it. She smiles.
O all of human wisdom seems to fall
into the reawakend depth of mystery.
She is the woman with the golden hair.

Her vulva gleams beneath the hairless mount of Venus.
It seems impenetrable in flesh or
as if some violence were needed of the man.

The mirror shines in a still of muted lust.
The image shows the oranges upon the ground
like jewels in the greeny gold of grass.

There is a plaintive singing in the air,
the air . . .   The daughters of Danaus fill
with blood the sieves of lust and cry.

THE REAPER

Created by the poets to sing my song,
or created by my song to sing.

The source of the song must die away.

All day the night of music hovers
in the fir-tree, swims and glitters.
O touch me not to song
for I desire to be forever mute with my first Lord.

The source of the song will die away.

Glorious is the hot sun.
The reaper in his youth cuts down the living grain.
We see the glitter of his hot curved scythe.
His weary labors cut us down
while yet we live.

The source of the song will die away.

Sweep not upon the strings of my dark lyre,
my body, music. Make mute
the tree within the heart, for I desire
to come unto my Lord unsung.

The Tomb of Muses in the marble of the flesh
is like a monument of song.

The source of the song will die away.

All night the pestilential reaper slays.
We fall away beneath his blade.
Our youth is daily harvested like wheat
from fields of our first Lord.

The source of the song will die away.

But see, glorious is the hot sun.
The Reaper cuts my hot youth down.
He cuts me down from my first Lord
while yet I live.

The source of the song will die away.

THE ADORATION OF THE VIRGIN

The speechless statue of the Virgin stands
among the whisperings of shadowy forms.
The magic beckoning extends
beyond her figure wrapt in the adoring light.
The solid druid wood, self-contain'd magic
of a live virginity, shows thru the gilt
the ruddy sheen of gold.

The poet lovers in the evening hall
walk in the clamor of dim carillons
that roll, that roll the fall of night.
They wait, disturb'd,
as if the rigid Virgin image were to stir
and speak. The miracle seems immanent.

She is not innocent, but, virgin,
she has known God. Her draperies

fly up, unfurl, and are caught
at war with the surrounding air,
carved in a wonder and brusht with gold.

To her, her son did not appear.
To us who did not know him
he appeard, white Baldur
in the bleeding wood appeard.

I walk with my lover. We sorrow for a third.
A third walks with us. Wounded splendor.
No longer mere, but changed. But more.
He bears our wounds, tears that are blood,
crowns that are thorns.

O haloed Mother, heal
my lover and myself. Hail
Mary full of grace.

The lonely image of the Virgin is
articulate with grace.
She holds the Infant Wizard
like an exclamation.

Forgive, forgive us in our love, and heal.

The druid wood disturbs.
It speaks beneath the leaf of gold.
Her woe is older than we know.
The gold, His blood, upon the rigid draperies,
gives grace.

The poet lovers feel her touch
as if that touch were stolen from their hearts.

HUON OF BORDEAUX

The torches in the windy corridors
light up their faces. One by one

the poets fall. Their faces
darken.

They are the legions of the Ruler of this World
and come to death. Their minds are vacant corridors
where winds may come from distances
and howl. Illuminations of no spirit.
No longer mere, there is something else.

I answer: *"This, Beloved,*
is to close the Happy Sphinx,
the statue half-emerging from the sea,
before whom let us gladly fail,
answer stupidly a question
answerd wisely might have forced
too early doom upon us."

The harpy lies in the slumbering waters,
glittering and pale,
and, like a sudden look into our own eyes,
we see her, mute, mad stone questioner.
We shall not hunger madly for a stone to speak.

Morgana le Fay! She is like a sphinx of stone,
or like a man
upon the throne of Christendom.
She stirs the fir-tree in her wise.

I feel Death's cold upon me when I see
the Tomb of Muses where the Lover lies.
He is a man surrounded by staves,
heir of imaginings, changeling son of a Roman king.

He, in all his brightness, has
cold memories of Egypt in his eyes.
He dreams of power not of love.
Conceived in a dark of power,
he will not die.

The empty armor of Ishkander Khan
casts its shade upon our bed.

We render unto Caesar what is Caesar's.
Our hearts are renderd to some spirit who has passt.
Our speech is renderd to the Riddler,
Our Lady of the Lake.

We listen, but we will not answer.
We will not speak forbidden things.
The Tomb of Muses where He lies
a sphinx's son of laughter,
floats upon the lethal sea.

THE ALBIGENSES

We move as dragons in the lethargy.
The spirit of our Lord moves in the universe
that spoke to us of evil things.
We hear the rustling of a serpent brilliance.

See how the worldly splendor swells.
The darkness of our Lord is vegetable with hate.

The spirits of the Light move in the dark.
They strive to touch. We know
dim memories of their chastity.

I know a serpent wisdom of the blood,
of suffering, of coital magic.
The light of our spirit is draind away
into the flesh. The womb,
the blood red sun, the universe,
are bright with evil presences,
angels of a leprous fire.

The spirit of desire moves in all lively things,
a beauty that glitters in the leaves of trees.

The Pope of Rome magnificent with massacres
is Lucifer. He repeats, repeats in us, creates
his evil image. The bride turns in the woe

of her devil's form and seeks to know
the devil maleness of her groom.
They eat the body of our Lord.
Golgotha mount stares on their paradise.

The poet lovers in copulation know
the emergence of the dragon from all things.
They burn in the wrath of the wrathful God.
Black is the beauty of the brightest day.

O let me die, but if you love me, let me die.
Your grief and fury hurt my second life.

I would come unto the source of light unsung.
The Golden Ones move in invisible realms.
If we could know their chastity. We strive to touch.
The consoled of God die away from life.
We reach, we reach to hold them back.
They grow invisible to our lust.

O let me die, but if you love me, let me die.

from *A Book of Resemblances* [1950–53]

THE HORNS OF ARTEMIS

There where great Artemis rides
naked, lake-clear bright lady
awakening her lovers, the hunters
    and the hunted,
her horns sound in the night.

Or are they horns of distant cars?
themselves fading and yet insistent,
that recall to the heart horns,
    trips made at night
    in indefinite longing,
or the betrayd lover's horns,
    painful crowns of the holy Moon.

We are awake now indeed,
And we are her Kings
    —fools poets and lunatics.

    Picture the Lady,
her whiplashes of pleasure, her bright
great eye fixt upon the games of the night.

    The bleeding bear
    and the hounds are one.
The enamord hunters ride themselves down.

    All love has fled.
    All lovers cower.
Only Truth remains, the eternal
    cold light shed on all things.

ADAM'S SONG

When this garden
is no longer home to us,
when we are
no longer at home in love
but restless,   and from faith
—mornings wide as a light room
and us light within the light
wherein bird-twitter at dawn
heralded green-leaf day—
when from the brightness of this day,
from faith's side,   we wake and find
our strangeness come with afternoon
—Eve, come with me beyond faith.

After the estranging apple at noon
in strangeness come with me.
We will come again to Paradise.
We will come again to rest
with eyes that have known unease,
falling away from the ripeness,
known rebellion,   exhaustion,
anger   •   return,
as if to the same place,
in another time
adore the restored garden.

And,   this is ours,   we will say.
As now we say this is ours,
seeing in the reflection of eyes
memory or promise of what we are,
as apples ripen in the eye
that meditates the flowering tree.
Or sees the fruit fall,
and the bare branch cries.

The war is all about us.   Our joy
is like a world to come
or a world past.   Near and far.

"Green-leaf day"   I said.
There is no more than
gold of your eye or
your lips smiling,   the
momentary curve,
to read love by.

This known wonder
returns, or we return to it.
As if rememberd, yet rare.
Never before known so.

Strangeness, come with me
beyond despair.   Beloved,
come with me.

It is as if the garden were
always there, even where we are,
here,   where war is,   the certain
end,   the paradise.

THE SONG OF THE BORDERGUARD

The man with his lion under the shed of wars
sheds his belief as if he shed tears.
The sound of words waits—
a barbarian host at the borderline of sense.

The enamord guards desert their posts
harkening to the lion-smell of a poem
that rings in their ears.

> —Dreams, a certain guard said—
> were never designd so
> to re-arrange an empire.

> Along about six o'clock I take out my guitar
> and sing to a lion

who sleeps like a line of poetry
in the shed of wars.

The man shedding his belief
knows that the lion is not asleep,
does not dream, is never asleep,
is a wide-awake poem
waiting like a lover for the disrobing of the guard;
the beautiful boundaries of the empire
naked, rapt round in the smell of a lion.

(The barbarians have passt over the significant phrase)

—When I was asleep,
    a certain guard says,
a man shed his clothes as if he shed tears
and appeard as a lonely lion
waiting for a song under the shed-roof of wars.

I sang the song that he waited to hear,
I, the Prize-Winner, the Poet-Acclaimd.

Dear, Dear, Dear, Dear, I sang,
believe, believe, believe, believe.
The shed of wars is splendid as the sky,
houses our waiting like a pure song
housing in its words the lion-smell
    of the beloved disrobed.

I sang: believe, believe, believe.

    I the guard because of my guitar
believe. I am the certain guard,
certain of the Beloved, certain of the Lion,
certain of the Empire. I with my guitar.
Dear, Dear, Dear, Dear, I sing.
I, the Prize-Winner, the Poet on Guard.

The borderlines of sense in the morning light
are naked as a line of poetry in a war.

A POEM IN STRETCHING

prophesying. Reading water or words, signs are cards in their multiple juxtapositions. Where we read into. Its not really there. Its nothing. A plate of disturbd sand. A landscape of sound, honks, sighs, a sigh. A plain stretch of time in which trees are not green but hesitate. A sign. The easy trees, houses, far away castles, a moat, a highway with car streams of, a high net of wires. It is nothing. Wires or eyes crosst giving rise to vision in the distortion of vision. Its not there. Its in the air. The rumor. It comes to our ears?

A poem stretching out once crampt in the hand. Heard having been seen. Now it is seen that it has been heard. A card, then another card. It is the queen of hearts and a seven. Black. Spades. Other cards we are not seeing determine the scene. We are not looking at them. We are not looking for them. They tell us, remind us. Unseen words we have just seen not yet heard tell us. I know now. I know, I mean. I see it all. All. She is afraid. A game of chance. Shuffle the deck. In the shuffle of words losing the sense we sense.

Put your cards on the table. O.K. Signs of the times.

A cigarette first. Yes. Hands in their motion holding.   A cigarette. Lighting. A match. Light cigarette. A hesitation. Pausing before striking. The hot smoke toxic we draw in. A gasp. Stop. A bitter gasp. The hand grasps the pencil, straining at the bite of the sharp lead leading. A gasp. A sigh. The hot smoke distracting the intractable mind.

I see it. I see it all the way thru to the next phrase.

*

A phrase of such beauty! A pity to mar it. Now, now. She is afraid. The other card, a pity. To mar it. Carving in a sense of flood of, an arrangement in flooding words. And we reach out in it all

> like a drunk man now swimming
> suspended, smoking,
> seeing at last the magical horizons
> the world is round around its roundness

contradicted. Everywhere.
An inspired mind could see it flat.
Suspended, gasping
in another element, lungs gasping
the hot smoke of vision,
a flat statement, a lasting doctrine.
Her husband has a collapsible hat.
Collapses.
An ending. A drunk man's words
doubling. An afflicted vision.
As flat as that.

POETRY DISARRANGED

Not a derangement of the senses but yes there is an occult other sense of meaning in all disarrangements Dis in his arranging means. What is it that I imagined the language to be? Not mythy except as there is the actual mythy evening, an atmosphere or preconception at best the darkness of the actual night. Not visionary except as the seen is real in its intensity—this is a scene word-wise. But a hut of words primitive to our nature. The language in its natural disarray.

Not being in history we see as living in and not upon the world. And the reader like a worried traveler might see "that little light in the vast dark forest" and come to our door, inquire within and sit for a night by the flickering of our sentences, hearing a tale nowheres about toward once upon we are telling. And it would be part of that realm of story that he might never find his way there again. Returning to find the place, he could no longer recognize his surroundings.

What I am picturing is a poetry spun out of an evening as a whole cloth spun out of a net of worn wool. And an out of the way, that everlasting cottage in the deepest part of the forest of the tales told by a fire. What I am picturing is an old shawl worn, of no earthly importance, a poetry reduced again to its threads. An evening entertainment of no great measure. Talk in a room we are going toward we were from. A secluded interrogation. Speech as if heard that it would not trouble the hearers were it unheard.

There can be no time for will or structural ambition, when one would listen only to the relative positions, lengths and divisions, clusters, interweavings and decisions.

A poet who sits in the light of words like a cat in the mote-filled sunlight of a window. Where he is in the sentence is there. And he listens as his poetry pictures his listening.

A BOOK OF RESEMBLANCES

There could be a book without nations in its chapters.

This would be portents that were portents of themselves. A constantly moving. This is as we ourselves are moving in coming and going, in sitting positions, knees crosst now, then legs wide apart planting their feet as our feet understanding.

There could be a story without its end in its unfolding.

This is on my mind. To stop even. Just as the rhythm. Just. In the divine outgrowing. To stop it. And restore the white vase. The separate flowers. These are flags. Our flags. One full, in papery lavender child and eager not yet full opening. One below, one above crumpling or and going limp in wet purples and sagging from color. Two curld buds, tight fists patient before flinging open.

A cat crossing the room. Stops. Rolls amorously. Eyes looking black in fullness. Narrowing. Rises. Licks paw. Lifts hind foot. Hugging leg over neck to lick, lick, lick like a dripping faucet the groin.

SALVAGES: AN EVENING PIECE

A plate in light upon a table is not a plate of hunger. Coins on the table have their own innocent glimmer. Everything about coins we obliterate in use and urgency. How lovely the silver dull disk glimmer is. Shells without remorse. The rubd antique nickle dated 1939 Liberty portrait relief of Jefferson and, beyond, darkend with use, a grimy patina beautiful 1929 buffalo Indian head nickle.

Bottles. An aluminum tea pot with wicker handle. A remnant length of Italian shawl worn by my grandmother in the 80s, this too, increasing as beauty in dimness. The reds, ochres, blacks and once perhaps almost white natural cotton yellowd. The wearing, the long use, the discoloring. It would be becoming to beauty in words worn out. As a poetry to be discolord.

It is not the age it is the wearing, it is the reversion of the thing from its values. One nickle, then two dimes brighter, a newness, fresh-minted (yet, when I look—in god we trust—it is 1944, the god is Mercury with winged helmet; the other, a bust of Deus Roosevelt roman style with sagging chin and stuck-up defiant nondescript head—this is 1947—in god we trust). Then two nickles, the grimy ones. One shiny fifty cent piece above. (Beyond) a fourth nickle showing Monticello E Pluribus Unum.

This mere ninety cents is more, is all piece by piece in art, as they are here, pieces of glimmer as rare as the mysterious chalice with faces and figures or the casting from the greek horse and rider.

Notes on use and values.

Then the litter. The gleams of silver and nickle seen as coins of light in the litter. A key, another gleam, an ancient evocation, a coin-silver spoon, a chipt cheap cup-shaped cup with a grey glaze without the imperfections of beauty beautiful because it is a cup. A large brown glass bottle of vitamins that look like beans. Papers. A letter from a friend, a program in my own script black and definite (defiant) arranged over the white paper. Matches. An envelope.

In the late hour left after the history of the day, taken with a will before bedtime—how transformd the world is! The silence almost reaches us in which an original, all that has been left behind, tosst about, of us remains.

Beautiful litter with thy gleam and glimmers, thy wastes and remains! The tide of our purpose has gone back into itself, into its own counsels. And it is the beauty of where we have been living that is the poetry of the hour.

from *Writing Writing* [1952–53]

THE BEGINNING OF WRITING

a composition

Beginning to write. Continuing finally to write. Writing finally to continue beginning.

To overcome the beginning. To overcome the urgency. To overcome writing in writing.

Not ever to overcome the beginning. Now to write writing. Not to overcome in beginning.

*

Love is sometimes advancing and including. Love is some times overcoming and not beginning. Love as a continual part of some writing is imagining expansion of loving to include beginning as continuing.

Desire : in not writing. Urgency : in not writing. Lying in waiting is not writing. Desire is the before not beginning of beginning. Urgency is a not feeling of finally beginning.

*

When I imagine not overcoming but including, loving takes place in the place of desiring. When I imagine daily beginning continuing, being is no longer re-forming but repeating.

A giant of the whole day is awakeness.
A giant of the whole night is sleeping.

To be a universe! To be a universe!
Wrapt in its continually speaking.
To be returnd to dreaming.

When I imagine myself as lover
Love is again here, here I say,
coming forth by Day once more
from all mere longing, belonging
to saying.
               The morning turns
quiet as words speaking,
a soliloquy of audible silence.

*

A soliloquy ! A soliloquy!
such idle talking in different colord lights, in sleights
of imagined person, in person.

The great Panjandrum rolls his eternal being like a drum
roll
over the measures of disorderd sleep.
Disorderd speech.

IMAGINING IN WRITING

Not in believing, but in pretending. Not in knowing, but in pretending.
Not in undergoing, but in pretending.

At last! At last! all of reality! We find we are only what we pretended to
be. We realize.

These lions in the lazy passages of time like poets surfeit themselves upon
carcasses of poetry.

*

He wants if he is there. He reaches,
almost. But touch touches.
He rises from touch enormous
shaking mere realities from his form
like an ocean on end, like a talking coffee pot at breakfast,
like an unbelievable story escaping the believing mind, a

criminal, a primitive, a demagogue, tyrant over the people,
an aroused automobile about to become an automobile.

He is so real that he longs for the real.
He grasps the idea. But touch touches.
And no mere idea, the ideal turns like a sleeping teacher
(another character) that renders
the whole act inconsequential. Magnificent shifts
of shiftless flesh. An armory of thighs, a pedagogy
of actual voluptuous pectoral pages to the hand,
words of hair, of visible eyes, closed or opend closing.
A foreign language.

*

How long at the corners of the street
the cars delay, we wait
for the promised, the promised,
for the promises that carry us home

away from the demands, the histories, away from the years.
Immortal, as in tears, we are carried. Away.

This is a description of sometimes a painful existing.
This is a description of a sometimes self betraying which is revealing.
This is a description in writing of the description in writing. This is a
scripture of a rapture in describing. In writing I am not but am writing.

This is a description of a continent of living: lions, streetcars, explosions,
newspapers like flies, flies like newspapers, giraffes of devotion, sen-
tences in locomotion as contrived as giraffes, as devoted as all passing
fashions. This is a description of passions designd as costumes of real
living.

This is a description of all pretend pages. Unimportant
magnificences of an inner forgiveness for living.

*

It is the measure of the crippled sentence. It is the pleasure of the poetry

rotting its words until the flesh of the language falls away from its bone.
It is the beautiful senseless tone in the language crippling the sentence.
The poetry. The stink of the real to the imaginary nose.
The skull is the rose. A face like all other faces unlike.
A finality. A betrayal.
The rows of uneven teeth like the measure of a sentence.

*

So we went up to the bedroom from all daily hungers and pleasures to
enter the dream, to enter together we said entwined as in death, as in
love, in unknowing otherness we anticipated, stretcht out each his own
eachness upon his own frame without space or time of stretching, chang-
ing and rechanging form, deformd, enormities of pitiful sleep.

The violence of a face cut open bleeding.
The violation of a form in a chin receding.
The violin of a figure disfigured for music, a crude
visual reminder, crackt, warpt, bloated.
An obscenity. A disemboweling.
A vile charm never to change changeling
strung like a skin over contradictory
skeletons of form.

We saw warts and corrosions dividing.
Diseases were only reminders of our dis-ease.

All that we disownd, we ownd,
until the sick lions climbing up from their mother-fucking
vomited the remains of all claimd pleasures.

WRITING AS WRITING

The word in the hand is the sound in the eye is the sight in the
listening ear. Listen, do you mind. Mind then the solid pattern of all this
soundless patter, collected together only in the writing.

The word has only been left on the page, left after the steady procession of developing sentences.

Poetry made up of sentences of words. Poetry in its regular irregular lines and divisions. Poetry in its steady revisions of its original vision, an accurate eye correcting its accuracies, an image of a man made in his own image inaccurately. I endeavor in delivering to deliver the speech from all truth spoken into its true form. I strive in inscribing in its different lengths the lengths of description I would go to, the lasts of all passages of literal understandings. I arrive in the reiteration of all the relations at lengthy vacations of ordinary prose in poses of poetry.

The word at rest rests in the mind in the restless continuation. The breaking down of all internal continual. The interruption of persistent locomotion. The persistent irruption of volcanic inconsequence. The landscape revised to portray a reality.

*

The landscape revised to portray a reality.
Seen from a height as heights of houses.
Seen as rows of intense cloud solid sounds.
Seen as a flat miasma of undiverted sunlight.
Seen as the intrusion of blue in the background,
        as blue in the foreground, crowded
        in a background of natural houses.
The city revised to outlast its sentences.

*

We see the architecture as a make shift reality, see sky as a poor part of nature, see the crowded clouds as a pleasure.

The design of the paragraffs is in totalities of of. A pure possession possesst in its illusive properties.

What do we know then but seeking to know the stretch and the shrinking, the sureness of aim and the aimless surety the feeling of security in reciting what we are doing, the fun of pursuing the ensuing phrases.

Opening our mouthed words to encompass the passage of time. Pretending the time in the space it takes to design our intentions. Relenting and preventing the importance of saying from satisfying and relaxing the hearer from listening. Relaxing the effort to fall back from its periods.

A literal transcription of letters is a conceit that pleases.

DESCRIPTIONS OF IMAGINARY POETRIES

1   Where giant wordlings interrupt the stuttering machine-gun wit; pale insensible bland body phrases loom, as islands in the line of fire. Not targets, but meaningless casualties. Luminous blobs in a splattered night scene; too accidental for inspiration, too clumsy for lyric.

2

      Gaps.
      Regular straining.
      Great rips in the febrile
      goods
      Gapes. A leftover intending.

3   My god, we thot after four minutes, how much more of this can there be? O a pure tedium. With and without ideas. A pure tedium.

4   The poet can barely lift these words. Not because they are heavy, but because he is so weak.

5   Unfolding phrases, like chairs closing into themselves. Furnitures walking, shifting sides over legs backs. A gate closed in order to open. Irregular measures of meaning. The words, all cream and curds, all slick and sheen.
      Drop and drop of acid. To permeate each custard area. A bitter cool smooth move ball bearing; a heavy wooden convertible structure.

6   A field of targets and archers. Bright black red and white concentric circles the bulls eyes. Looking not watching. Sing sting sing slings and arrows of fortune. Birds fly far afield in faroff sky. A shout arises. Almost. Haloo! Elegiac victories.

And all this refers to one's extreme of youth. How extreme youth is.

7   Wide awake confusions.
Then drowsy illness. Ill, at ease.
Then—deep imageless sequence of words as blackout.
Confused, aroused;
two words startled like deep sleeping deer started up from deep thicket of words
aroused, confusion, like the breaking and smashing and trampling of a thicket of words. A weary after statement of wide awake confused aroused.

8   Two or three occasional
endearing clear
statement of a tea pot, a
sculptural head, a cat asleep.

from *Letters* [1953–56]

FOR A MUSE MEANT

: in
   s p i r e d /the aspirate
   the aspirant almost

   without breath

  it is a breath out
   breathed—an aspiration
  pictured as the familiar spirit
  hoverer
     above
  each loved each

  a word giving up its ghost
   memorized as the flavor
     from the vowels (the bowels)
     of meaning
(BE STILL THY BRATHE AND HEAR THEM SPEAK:)
voices? images? essences
   as only in
Yeats's 'desolation of reality'.

hesitate (as if the
bone-cranium-helmet
in-bearing); clearing
old greym attar.

:   specialization, yes. Better to stum-
  b'l to it. You cld have
  knockd me over with a feather weight
  of words. The sense
  sleight but absolute.
  nock. nock. nock sum sense into me head.
   O K
  Better awake to it. For one
   eyes-wide-open vision

or fotograf.
Than ritual.

Specialization,—yes even if the old ritual
is lost.(*)

    I was completely lost and saw the sign
    without meaning to.
    This was not the design.

:   A great effort, straining, breaking up
all the melodic line   (the lyr-
ick strain?)   Dont
hand me that old line we say
You dont know what yer saying.

    Why knot ab   stract
    a tract of   mere sound
    is more   a round
    of dis abs cons
       t r a c t i o n
    —a deconstruction—
    for the reading of words.

Lists of imaginary sounds I mean sound signs I mean things designd in
themselves I mean boundary marks I mean a bounding memorizations I
mean a memorial rising I mean

a con glomerations without rising

    1. a dead camel
    2. a nude tree
    3. a hot mouth (smoking)

(*) *Who works at his own word in all of our sentences might trick from even the ruts of once ritual the buts and mistakes that token the actual. The true poet as maker frees the thing from its prophets.*

4. an old saw (rusty edge)
5. a copy of the original
6. an animal face
7. a broken streetcar
8. a fake seegar
9. papers
10. a holey shawl
11. the addition of the un
    plannd for interruption:
    a flavor stinking coffee
    (how to brew another cup
    in that Marianne Moore–
    E.P.–Williams-H.D.–Stein–
    Zukofsky–Stevens–Perse–
    surrealist–dada–staind
    pot)   by yrs R.D.
12. a table set for break
    fast

    a morning lang
    wage—AI AI a-wailing
       the failing

FOR A SONG OF THE LANGUAGERS

What are the signs of life? the breath, the pulse,
   the constant
sluffing off of old stuff in
    creasing, increasing—
   Notes: to hesitate, retract.
    Step by
             /to be idiot-awkward
      step

               to take care
   by the throat & throttle it.

    Bottle that genius
for mere magic or intoxic
        vacations.

  It is sober he stumbles
    on truth? Hell, no—
this he sober gnaws
the inconsequential
      eternity of his skull.

  His appetite is not experimental.

UPON TAKING HOLD

  the world as we reach stretches,
      a hand in sight.
Thumb, Mountain, Tidelands of Lines,
      the heart and head lines,
the palmist said—stars,
        shatterings from Moon
                          to
                  slumbering Venus.

Mt Tamalpais.

    Cézanne restored the destroyd mountain.
And the hand in the painting
      comes up from its illusions
—a man shaped to the world's fate
      stretches upon his face

to wear the given mask.
Shaking himself from his wars,
      a ready dog.
It is to grasp or to measure
      a hand's breadth,

>   this hand—mine
>   as I write—
> dares its contradictions,
>   comes to rest,
> tenses, shakes, seizes or is seized by the mind:
>
>   mind, hand, eye,
>
> moves over the keys.   It is the exercise.
> The poetry—now—a gesture,
> a lifting of sentence as the wind lifts,
> palm outward in address,
>   fingers
>   exactly
>   curld
>
>   —it is a fact—
>
> the words not to be alterd.
>
> Is there another altar than the fact we make,
> the form, fate, future dared
>   desired in the act?
>
> Words can drop as my hand drops (hawk
>   on wing
>   waits
>   weight and
>   drops
> to conquer inarticulate love
>   leaving articulate
>
>   the actual mountain.
>
> This is the bunch of ranunculus,
>   rose, butter, orange crowfoot
>   profuse bouquet in its white china pitcher;
> this is the hookd rug workd in rich color
>   the red, blue, ochre,

violet, emerald, azure,
the black, pink, rose,
oyster white, the orange . . .
this is the orange measurement of the lines
 as I design them.
The joys of the household are fates that command us.

FIRST INVENTION ON THE THEME OF THE ADAM

1. The streets. Of the mind. Whose gangs
of who in the whom of avenues hooing
passt? They wrote parts of color.
Each as the Anthropos
swallowing himself in continual likeness.
Who? Who?
      the streets ring out
 and are cleard, swept by noises.
What gangsters in whose anger
 arousing.
    The sweep of his never reaching
reminds us. Brought to our beds
under an idea. Released
 crowds traffic conglomerations.

She was white whippt and complete
 as we saw her.

She was one like of him.

2. In the before streets, the streets occurrd.
A mind, crowded to be seen. A maker
occurring only to the created.
It is the howl that arises that acclaims him.
 He is as he is
they did not know as they saw him.

3. The blindness of the mountain.   O
our mountainous eye. Watch
us. Clock us. Clock us.
> Hand over hand over us.   Sur-
> rounding the hour of our end
>> in surrounding.

4. He was one like him that in grown out cast over bearing under done
far fetchd near by all most quite all ways never with out full filld part time
close spaced semi-literate multi-phase of a face of him her.
She was one like her in the hymn to our load as we carry him
where we in our herd are halving our going.

> 5. The voices in the dark in the place of stars.
> The starting up in the dark in the place of lying still.
> The still dark in the place where the stars displace the lying voices.
> Old Mother Anthropos
> refuses to face her hour's mirror.
> You know her. She lives in the shoe
>> that fits her.
> Who. Who. She hears in the mountain
>> (a gangster voice in a street to come).
> Knows what to do. Who. Who.
> Knows in the too many of her.
>> What to do.

LIGHT SONG

> ; husbands   the hand   the keys   a free imp-
>> rovisation keeping the constant vow,
>>> a music,
> with set conjugations, notes, the light-
>> est estimations of ravishd ear
> naturally contrived.   The contrivance
>> vanishes into itself.

     Thus law:
It is this music that the composer dares,
  plays, percussively,
  the state I love. A
    volition.
  To seize from the air its forms.

This longing informs. A declaration—
   Lawrence: LOOK WE HAVE COME THRU.
   Pound: IT ALL COHERES. A SPLENDOUR.
where the spirit of the act appears eve-
  n ruthless. This
  is the inevitable beauty.

; husbands by hand upon the keys unlock
   from all compulsions—a mode.
It is wed so seven pastorals Harrison playd.

  It was the wellwise where intellect
  that Dante saw as God—a rose—
  Vanzetti beyond the Miseria saw
   a voluntary state.
        The Bride:
  wed as we move to that we await.

     •

And the rhyme waits for us, a beloved
   won as she wins us.
I give up my poet into the tongues.
   She that very Sancta Sophia it is
   pictured at San Vitale
in gold, mother-of-pearl, vermillion, purple,

   word by word, appears
the Empress Theodora Procopius
   saw was whore
faces the poet Emperor her eternal

husband
witness
paramour.

It is as the artist wrought it.
        All things hierarchically are
                ranged:
The Divine Garbo has appeard in her guise;
Chaplin Lawrence said was beauty in a man
        in 'City Lights'
the silent moving picture speech or
indistinguishable metropolis murmuring a loud
        we do not hear
                        suggests
        the language we long for.
                        Hidden.

As in the measures the song is hidden.
        Heard as we sing her
word upon word.   The design

                as we observe it.

IT'S SPRING. LOVE'S SPRING.

                        The April stirring
        not to be denied. Inert
        wonderings try me.
And I am very Death that lusts after all men;
that straight and crooked draws into his ken
        all bright live eyes
        to wive. Avidly.
The mind possesses them. Another life!
To trick the inevitable weather.
To spring the catch: but the catch
        springs up from the song
long as the year, an engagement, lifelasting,
        even distracted . . .

It is a melody skirted, a configuration
        —as in Schönberg's Serenade—
a blossoming in shame, almost seen
        or heard, but never . . .

an exact other melody of the strings
        that art refuses to render
        useful.
And so—unrenderd—
        we are torn apart
—as April rips the weather of our hearts—
        longing from longing:
we could not afford,   or lovewise devise
        the cost
        that sustains us.

TRUE TO LIFE

6/20   went
  up to the Denials of Poetry: those Dames
Poe saw who combd their brassy hair and sang.

That was the corruption of an imaginary Rome.

To force a saying out of obscure need
costs we cannot afford to avoid: even it be bad
and fall apart.
               St Augustine's stylewise
war to mar all elegance—   How? be ignorant?
It needs the flint hard edge of recalcitrant almost
    hatred of truth   to strike
light of denied long-desired otherness.   A truth!

St Gregory the Great's miracles are lies; his lies
    his miracles.

If the mind can devise just such an eight hundred years old
                      [tortoise six feet in diameter
clambering over the explorer's view, his wonder itself makes
                          [him authentic.

6/24   *My not getting at my dreams is part of not coming to grips with life;*
which would, is, protean, be multiform. Energies there (inner as dreams, outer
as events) or energy in the correspondence. But the attempt to get at the dream
again would mean, seem to be, confessional, a self-exposure. Is my hypocrisy so
pervasive?

6/27   Breaks in the discourse disclose
    rifts of determination,
                            an effort of mind.
The adamant sphinx immediacy
demands a simple riddle
                        out of my crowded sense?
Sweep clear to a singing true thing!
    Thus: it is the block in view blesses,
restores. . .

What do you do if the recalcitrant incoherence
    is riddled thru with feeling?
There is no starting or stopping there—
no abrupt courageous facing of a fact,
    lion-bodied female-visaged actual other
        to question.
                        Dreaming or awake
    the facts seem to lie about to speak
a gift of tongues.   Only the free
        medium,
the speech, rings
    —If I could hear aright? by waiting?—
        rings true.

To dispell shadows of meaning
revealing inconsequent things,

        the immediate empire.

THE HUMAN COMMUNION. TRACES.

                                The dead
are the departed therefrom.   Whose
leavings.   Reading we partake of.

A lamp of letters,   a ladder of
                divine signs,
a substance of ourselves lost, lost
in a world lost waste lost that we must gather
                out.

        Set like a crying girl to sift cinders
out of old passions.   For a first fire.
    For a light in old age to burn in the skull
        that lit youth's loins?
    Covetous brain!

        But read further,   read further.
Beloved Shakespeare,   beloved Lao Tse,
        beloved Virginia Woolf!
    My heart is submerged as I read.

        Above:
        the swarming radiance.

These that I never saw I see.

        Below:
        the boundless waters.

RE-

-turn.   In spring-up green freshet
turn.   Delight to the eye,   spring
to torso,   hand spring to wheel,
thigh turn upon thigh;
eye light to eye;   heart

-bound as we are bound to return,
        however casually,
to time or place instinct for joy:
measures wither or rot
        of habitual conflict.
Old theme of poetry!   heart worn

were it not the source
contrary to all weariness.

Thus from the lusty stalk whose green
                          tips
turns bud blast to full bloom that
love in desire makes its brief room.

         Again and again.

Worm, like an ideology, he eats of the core.
Aphids, like retractions, devour.
Grass, bush or tree in flower
          serves as reminder.

-wind, old theme of the poem,   step to step
                          dance to
the rewinding measures
                          the fresh shoots of war.

SOURCE

   Or: I work at the language as a spring of water works at the rock, to
find a course, and so, blindly. In this I am not a maker of things, but, if
maker, a maker of a way. For the way in itself. It is well enuf to speak of
water's having its destination in the sea, and so to picture almost a know-
ing in the course; but the sea is only the end of ways—could the stream
find a further course, it would go on. And vast as the language is, it is no
end but a resistance thru which a poem might move—as it flows or
dances or puddles in time—making it up in its going along and yet going
only as it breaks the resistance of the language.
   When I was about twelve—I suppose about the age of Narcissus—I
fell in love with a mountain stream. There, most intensely for a summer,
staring into its limpid cold rush, I knew the fullest pain of longing. To be
of it, entirely, to be out of my being and enter the Other clear impossible
element. The imagination, old shape-shifter, stretcht itself painfully to
comprehend the beloved form.
   Then all windings and pools, all rushings on, constant inconstancy,
all streams out of springs we do not know where, all rush of senses and

intellect thru time of being—lifts me up; as if out of the pulse of my bloody flesh, the gasp of breath upon breath (like a fish out of water) there were another continuum, an even-purling stream, crystal and deep, down there, but a flow of waters.

I write this only to explain some of the old ache of longing that revives when I apprehend again the currents of language—rushing upon their way, or in pools, vacant energies below meaning, hidden to our purposes. Often, reading or writing, the fullest pain returns, and I see or hear or almost know a pure element of clearness, an utter movement, an absolute rush along its own way, that makes of even the words under my pen a foreign element that I may crave—as for kingdom or salvation or freedom—but never know.

OFTEN I AM PERMITTED TO RETURN TO A MEADOW

as if it were a scene made-up by the mind,
that is not mine, but is a made place,

that is mine, it is so near to the heart,
an eternal pasture folded in all thought
so that there is a hall therein

that is a made place, created by light
wherefrom the shadows that are forms fall.

Wherefrom fall all architectures I am
I say are likenesses of the First Beloved
whose flowers are flames lit to the Lady.

She it is Queen Under The Hill
whose hosts are a disturbance of words within words
that is a field folded.

It is only a dream of the grass blowing
east against the source of the sun
in an hour before the sun's going down

whose secret we see in a children's game
of ring a round of roses told.

Often I am permitted to return to a meadow
as if it were a given property of the mind
that certain bounds hold against chaos,

that is a place of first permission,
everlasting omen of what is.

THE STRUCTURE OF RIME I

I ask the unyielding Sentence that shows Itself forth in the language
as I make it,

> Speak!   For I name myself your master, who come to serve.
> Writing is first a search in obedience.

There is a woman who resembles the sentence. She has a place in mem-
ory that moves language. Her voice comes across the waters from a shore
I don't know to a shore I know, and is translated into words belonging to
the poem:

> *Have heart*, the text reads,
>   *you that were heartless.*
> *Suffering joy or despair*
> *you will suffer the sentence*
> *a law of words moving*
> *seeking their right period.*

I saw a snake-like beauty in the living changes of syntax.

> *Wake up*, she cried.
> *Jacob wrestled with Sleep—you who fall into Nothingness*
>   *and dread sleep.*
> *He wrestled with Sleep like a man reading a strong*
>   *sentence.*

I will not take the actual world for granted, I said.

> *Why not?* she replied.
> *Do I not withhold the song of birds from you?*
> *Do I not withhold the penetrations of red from you?*
> *Do I not withhold the weight of mountains from you?*
> *Do I not withhold the hearts of men from you?*

> *I alone long for your demand.*
> *I alone measure your desire.*

O Lasting Sentence,
sentence after sentence I make in your image. In the feet that measure
the dance of my pages I hear cosmic intoxications of the man I will be.

>   *Cheat at this game?* she cries.
>   *The world is what you are.*
>   *Stand then*
>   *so I can see you, a fierce destroyer of images.*

>   *Will you drive me to madness*
>   *only there to know me?*
>   *vomiting images into the place of the Law!*

THE STRUCTURE OF RIME II

What of the Structure of Rime? I said.

The Messenger in guise of a Lion roard: *Why does man retract his song
from the impoverishd air? He brings his young to the opening of the field. Does
he so fear beautiful compulsion?*

I in the guise of a Lion roard out great vowels and heard their amazing
patterns.

A lion without disguise said: He that sang to charm the beasts was false of
tongue. There is a melody within this surfeit of speech that is most man.
What of the Structure of Rime? I asked.

*An absolute scale of resemblance and disresemblance establishes measures
that are music in the actual world.*

The Lion in the Zodiac replied:

*The actual stars moving are music in the real world. This is the meaning of
the music of the spheres.*

THE STRUCTURE OF RIME IV

    O Outrider!
               when you come to the threshold of the stars,
to the door beyond which moves celestial terror—

    the kin at the hearth, the continual cauldron that feeds forth the
earth, the heart that comes into being through the blood, the house-
holder among his familiar animals, the beloved turning to his beloved in
the dark

        create love as the leaves
        create from the light   life
and return to the remote precincts where the courageous move
ramifications of the unknown that appear as trials.

    The Master of Rime, time after time, came down the arranged lad-
ders of vision or ascended the smoke and flame towers of the opposite of
vision, into or out of the language of daily life, husband to one word, wife
to the other, breath that leaps forward upon the edge of dying.

    Thus I said to the source of my happiness, I will return. From the
moment of your love eternity expands, and you are mere man.

        water   fire   earth   and air
        all that simple elements were

        guardians are.

THE STRUCTURE OF RIME VI

    The old women came from their caves to close the too many doors
that lead into pastures. Thru which the children pass, and in the high
grass build their rooms of green, kingdoms where they dwell under the
will of grasshopper, butterfly, snail, quail, thrush, mole and rabbit.

    *Old Woman, your eye searches the field like a scythe! The riches of the
living green lie prepared for your store. Ah, but you come so near to the*

children! you have almost returnd to them. Their voices float up from their
faraway games where. The tunneld grass hides their clearings. Swords and
blades cut the near blue of sky. Their voices surround you.

    Old Woman, at last you have come so near you almost understand them.

    Have you recalld then how the soul floats as the tiger-tongued butterfly or
that sapphire, the humming-bird, does, where it will?

Lying in the grass, the world was all of the field, and I saw a kite on its
string, tugging, bounding—far away as my grandmother—dance against
the blue from its tie of invisible delight.

    In the caves of blue within the blue the grandmothers bound, on the
brink of freedom, to close the too many doors from which the rain falls.

    Thus, the grass must give up new keys to rescue the living.

THIS PLACE RUMORD TO HAVE BEEN SODOM

    might have been.
Certainly these ashes might have been pleasures.
Pilgrims on their way to the Holy Places remark
this place. Isn't it plain to all
that these mounds were palaces? This was once
a city among men, a gathering together of spirit.
It was measured by the Lord and found wanting.

It was measured by the Lord and found wanting,
destroyd by the angels that inhabit longing.
Surely this is Great Sodom where such cries
as if men were birds flying up from the swamp
ring in our ears, where such fears that were once
desires walk, almost spectacular,
stalking the desolate circles, red eyed.

This place rumord to have been a City surely was,
separated from us by the hand of the Lord.
The devout have laid out gardens in the desert,
drawn water from springs where the light was blighted.

How tenderly they must attend these friendships
or all is lost. All *is* lost.
Only the faithful hold this place green.

Only the faithful hold this place green
where the crown of fiery thorns descends.
Men that once lusted grow listless. A spirit
wrappd in a cloud, ashes more than ashes,
fire more than fire, ascends.
Only these new friends gather joyous here,
where the world like Great Sodom lies under fear.

The world like Great Sodom lies under Love
and knows not the hand of the Lord that moves.
This the friends teach where such cries
as if men were birds fly up from the crowds
gatherd and howling in the heat of the sun.
In the Lord Whom the friends have named at last Love
the images and loves of the friends never die.
This place rumord to have been Sodom is blessd
in the Lord's eyes.

THE BALLAD OF THE ENAMORD MAGE

How the Earth turns round under the Sun I know,
And how the Numbers in the Constellations glow,
How all Forms in Time will grow
And return to their single Source
Informd by Grief, Joy, insatiable Desire
And cold Remorse.

Serpents I have seen bend the Evening Air
Where Flowers that once Men and Women were
Voiceless spread their innocent Lustre.
I have seen green Globes of Water
Enter the Fire. In my Sight
Tears have drownd the Flames of Animal Delight.

I, a poor writer, who knows not
where or wherefor my body was begot.

In a World near a City in a green Tree
I was once a Bird shot down by Thee.
And Thou, Beloved, shot from Thy young Bow
An Arrow from which my Blood doth daily flow
And stoppd the Song
That now I sing Thee all Night long.

    I, turning my verse, waiting for the rime,
    that know not the meaning of my name.

In a place where a Stone was, hot in the Sun,
I was once a Mage, dry as a Bone,
And calld to me a Demon of myself alone
Who from my Thirst conjured a green River
And out of my Knowledge I saw Thee run,
A Spring of pure Water.

    I, late at night, facing the page
    writing my fancies in a literal age.

How all beings into all beings pass,
How the great Beasts eat the human Grass,
And the Faces of Men in the Word's Glass
Are faces of Apes, Birds, Diamonds,
Worlds and insubstantial Shapes
Conjured out of the Dust—Alas!
These things I know.
Worlds out of Worlds in Magic grow.

    I, mortal, that live by chance,
    and know not why you love,
    praise the great wheel where the spirits dance,
    for by your side I move.

THE MAIDEN

                              we consider
precedent to that Shekinah,   She
in whom the Jew has his communion.
Lovely to look at,   modesty
imparts to her nakedness willowy
grace. Bright with spring,   *vestita*
di nobilissimo colore umile ed onesto sanguigno
Dante saw her   *so that the heart trembled.*
In Hell   Persephone showd
brightness of death her face, spring
slumbering.
                    Came to that spring,
or is attendant there, to draw water:
thus, Rachel, *dal principio del suo anno nono,*
a girl, lifted to Jacob's dry mouth
her cup that fed his manhood's thirst.
Because we thirst for clarity,
the crystal clear brook Undine wakes
unquenchable longing, in which
jewels innocent show in lovely depths.

    Her persistence makes
Freud's teaching that a child has sexual phantasies
terrible. Yellowy green that breaks winter
of daffodil or asphodel, witch's color
(but to Wordsworth's natural heart epiphany)
Ophelia wore, heart's rendering.
Hamlet, Edith Sitwell tells us was dark earth, cries
"Get thee to a nunnery!" Ophelia grieves
for her dead Father, the old year
thrown aside. "The little Fertility ghost or Vegetation demon,
ghost of Spring, casts herself into the stream
wreathed with flowers." Another maiden,
Elizabeth Eleanor Siddal in a silvery dress
"drowning for an hour or so" posed for Millais
to capture a wild chastity. And Bonnard
teaches us again and again   where she appears

reflecting watery blues and greens in tiled bathrooms
a wife may be   maiden to the eye.

> No goddess, She
> must be revived,
> Cora among the grasses.
> Hearts
> revive with her.

> Memory
> holds particular maidens
> inviolate
> and quickens
> as if Spring had arrived

> when in an elderly maiden's face
> (Marianne Moore's)
> the camera shows
> penetrating beauty
> and Her grace.

The old say they are young in heart.   Youth
is part of power in the thriving shoot
the earnest begonia forces toward the sun.
When illness overtook her, Mrs Adam
dwelt in her girlhood and heard
music from a piano that was not here,
strains of sixty years ago.
Her mind was wandering.   It is well
of water we return to.

Men have mothers.   They are of women born
and from this womanly knowledge
womanly, but Christ
was more and rare that was a maiden's Babe:
He was part girl.   He had solitude.

Because it is Mystery, such puberty
counterfeited in simpering coy glances, piety,
        giggles, girlish attitudes,

is loathsome, contaminated water, field
    desecrated by picnickers.

It is the girl the man knows nothing of.
His heart stops short and must
belong to her by trust he knows as pain:
    —*quando m'apparve Amor subitamente,*
thus Dante Alighieri gaind New Life,
therein Love apprehended. "The pain of loving you,"
Lawrence writes, "is almost more than I can bear . . .
I live in fear." *Donna della salute!*

Fear is a flame in your propriety.

   The Close

Close to her construct I pace the line,
the containd homage arranged, reflections
on Marianne Moore's natural style, an artifice
where sense may abound. As in a photograph of her
I found the photographer with his camera had caught
artfully a look where this flame took my mind
of beauty in which a maiden's
unlikely hardihood may be retaind.

POETRY, A NATURAL THING

    Neither our vices nor our virtues
further the poem. "They came up
    and died
just like they do every year
    on the rocks."

    The poem
feeds upon thought, feeling, impulse,
    to breed   itself,
a spiritual urgency at the dark ladders leaping.

This beauty is an inner persistence
    toward the source

striving against (within) down-rushet of the river,
    a call we heard and answer
in the lateness of the world
    primordial bellowings
from which the youngest world might spring,

salmon not in the well where the
    hazelnut falls
but at the falls battling, inarticulate,
    blindly making it.

This is one picture apt for the mind.

A second: a moose painted by Stubbs,
where last year's extravagant antlers
    lie on the ground.
The forlorn moosey-faced poem wears
    new antler-buds,
    the same,

"a little heavy, a little contrived",

his only beauty to be
    all moose.

A POEM BEGINNING WITH A LINE BY PINDAR

I

The light foot hears you and the brightness begins
god-step at the margins of thought,
    quick adulterous tread at the heart.
Who is it that goes there?
    Where I see your quick face
notes of an old music pace the air,
torso-reverberations of a Grecian lyre.

In Goya's canvas Cupid and Psyche
have a hurt voluptuous grace
bruised by redemption. The copper light
falling upon the brown boy's slight body

is carnal fate that sends the soul wailing
up from blind innocence, ensnared
    by dimness
into the deprivations of desiring sight.

But the eyes in Goya's painting are soft,
diffuse with rapture absorb the flame.
Their bodies yield out of strength.
    Waves of visual pleasure
wrap them in a sorrow previous to their impatience.

A bronze of yearning, a rose that burns
    the tips of their bodies, lips,
ends of fingers, nipples. He is not wingd.
His thighs are flesh, are clouds
    lit by the sun in its going down,
hot luminescence at the loins of the visible.

    But they are not in a landscape.
    They exist in an obscurity.

The wind spreading the sail serves them.
The two jealous sisters eager for her ruin
    serve them.
That she is ignorant, ignorant of what Love will be,
    serves them.
The dark serves them.
The oil scalding his shoulder serves them,
serves their story. Fate, spinning,
    knots the threads for Love.

Jealousy, ignorance, the hurt . . . serve them.

II

This is magic. It is passionate dispersion.
What if they grow old? The gods
    would not allow it.
    Psyche is preserved.

In time we see a tragedy, a loss of beauty
    the glittering youth
of the god retains—but from this threshold
    it is age
that is beautiful. It is toward the old poets
    we go, to their faltering,
their unaltering wrongness that has style,
    their variable truth,
    the old faces,
words shed like tears from
a plenitude of powers time stores.

A stroke.   These little strokes.   A chill.
    The old man, feeble, does not recoil.
Recall. A phase so minute,
    only a part of the word in- jerrd.

    The Thundermakers descend,

damerging a nuv. A nerb.
    The present dented of the U
nighted stayd.   States.   The heavy clod?
    Cloud.   Invades the brain.   What
    if lilacs last in *this* dooryard bloomd?

Hoover, Roosevelt, Truman, Eisenhower—
where among these did the power reside
that moves the heart? What flower of the nation
bride-sweet broke to the whole rapture?
Hoover, Coolidge, Harding, Wilson
hear the factories of human misery turning out commodities.
For whom are the holy matins of the heart ringing?
Noble men in the quiet of morning hear
Indians singing the continent's violent requiem.
Harding, Wilson, Taft, Roosevelt,
idiots fumbling at the bride's door,
hear the cries of men in meaningless debt and war.
Where among these did the spirit reside
that restores the land to productive order?
McKinley, Cleveland, Harrison, Arthur,

Garfield, Hayes, Grant, Johnson,
dwell in the roots of the heart's rancor.
How sad "amid lanes and through old woods"
  echoes Whitman's love for Lincoln!

There is no continuity then.   Only a few
    posts of the good remain.   I too
that am a nation sustain the damage
    where smokes of continual ravage
obscure the flame.
                It is across great scars of wrong
  I reach toward the song of kindred men
  and strike again the naked string
old Whitman sang from.   Glorious mistake!
  that cried:

  "The theme is creative and has vista."
  "He is the president of regulation."

I see always the under side turning,
fumes that injure the tender landscape.
  From which up break
lilac blossoms of courage in daily act
  striving to meet a natural measure.

III   (for Charles Olson)

                  Psyche's tasks—the sorting of seeds
wheat   barley   oats   poppy   coriander
anise   beans   lentils   peas   —every grain
            in its right place
                  before nightfall;

gathering the gold wool from the cannibal sheep
(for the soul must weep
  and come near upon death);

harrowing Hell for a casket Proserpina keeps
                that must not
  be opend . . . containing beauty?
no!   Melancholy coild like a serpent

                          that is deadly sleep
we are not permitted
          to succumb to.

    These are the old tasks.
    You've heard them before.

    They must be impossible. Psyche
must despair, be brought to her
                    insect instructor;
must obey the counsels of the green reed;
saved from suicide by a tower speaking,
    must follow to the letter
    freakish instructions.

In the story the ants help. The old man at Pisa
    mixd in whose mind
(to draw the sorts) are all seeds
      as a lone ant from a broken ant-hill
had part restored by an insect, was
    upheld by a lizard

          (to draw the sorts)
the wind is part of the process
          defines a nation of the wind—

    father of many notions,
                 Who?
let the light into the dark?   began
the many movements of the passion?

                  West
from east   men push.
           The islands are blessd
(cursed)   that swim below the sun,

  man upon whom the sun has gone down!

There is the hero who struggles east
widdershins to free the dawn   and must

woo Night's daughter,
sorcery, black passionate rage, covetous queens,
so that the fleecy sun go   back from Troy,
        Colchis, India . . . all the blazing armies
spent, he must struggle alone toward the pyres of Day.

The light that is Love
rushes on toward passion. It verges upon dark.
        Roses and blood flood the clouds.
        Solitary first riders advance into legend.

This land, where I stand, was all legend
in my grandfathers' time: cattle raiders,
        animal tribes, priests, gold.
It was the West. Its vistas painters saw
        in diffuse light, in melancholy,
in abysses left by glaciers as if they had been the sun
        primordial carving empty enormities
                        out of the rock.

Snakes lurkd
guarding secrets.   Those first ones
                        survived solitude.

Scientia
holding the lamp, driven by doubt;
Eros naked in foreknowledge
smiling in his sleep;   and the light
spilld, burning his shoulder—the outrage
        that conquers legend—
passion, dismay, longing, search
        flooding up where
the Beloved is lost.   Psyche travels
life after life, my life, station
        after station,
to be tried

        without break, without
news, knowing only—but what did she know?
        The oracle at Miletus had spoken

truth surely: that he was Serpent-Desire
        that flies thru the air,
a monster-husband. But she saw him fair

whom Apollo's mouthpiece said spread
        pain
beyond cure   to those
        wounded by his arrows.

Rilke torn by a rose thorn
blackend toward Eros.   Cupidinous Death!
        that will not take no for an answer.

IV

        Oh yes!   Bless the footfall where
step by step   the boundary walker
(in Maverick Road   the snow
thud by thud   from the roof
circling the house—another tread)

    that foot   informd
by the weight of all things
        that can be elusive
no more than a nearness to the mind
        of a single image

        Oh yes!   this
most dear
        the catalyst force that renders clear
the days of a life from the surrounding medium!

        Yes, beautiful rare wilderness!
wildness that verifies strength of my tame mind,
        clearing held against indians,
health that prepared to meet death,
        the stubborn hymns going up
into the ramifications of the hostile air

        that, deceptive, gives way.

Who is there?   O, light the light!
    The Indians give way,   the clearing falls.
Great Death gives way   and unprepares us.
    Lust gives way.   The Moon gives way.
Night gives way.   Minutely,   the Day gains.

She saw the body of her beloved
    dismemberd in waking . . . or was it
in sight?   *Finders Keepers* we sang
    when we were children   or were taught to sing
before our histories began   and we began
    who were beloved   our animal life
toward the Beloved,   sworn to be Keepers.

    On the hill before the wind came
the grass moved toward the one sea,
    blade after blade dancing in waves.

There the children turn the ring to the left.
There the children turn the ring to the right.
    Dancing . . . Dancing . . .

And the lonely psyche goes up thru the boy to the king
    that in the caves of history dreams.
Round and round the children turn.
    London Bridge that is a kingdom falls.

We have come so far that all the old stories
whisper once more.
Mount Segur, Mount Victoire, Mount Tamalpais . . .
    rise to adore the mystery of Love!

(An ode? Pindar's art, the editors tell us, was not a statue but a
mosaic, an accumulation of metaphor. But if he was archaic, not
classic, a survival of obsolete mode, there may have been old
voices in the survival that directed the heart. So, a line from a
hymn came in a novel I was reading to help me. Psyche, poised
to leap—and Pindar too, the editors write, goes too far, topples
over—listend to a tower that said, *Listen to Me!* The oracle
had said, *Despair! The Gods themselves abhor his power.* And

then the virgin flower of the dark falls back flesh of our flesh
from which everywhere . . .

    the information flows
      that is yearning. A line of Pindar
    moves from the area of my lamp
      toward morning.

    In the dawn that is nowhere
      I have seen the willful children

    clockwise and counter-clockwise turning.

THE STRUCTURE OF RIME XI

There are memories everywhere then. Rememberd, we go out, as in
the first poem, upon the sea at night—to the drifting.

Of my first lover there is a boat drifting. The oars have been cast down
into the shell. As if this were no water but a wall, there is a repeated
knock as of hollow against hollow, wood against wood. Stooping to knock
on wood against the traps of the nightfishers, I hear before my knocking
the sound of a knock drifting.

It goes without will thru the perilous sound, a white sad wanderer
where I no longer am. It taps at the posts of the deserted wharf.

Now from the last years of my life I hear forerunners of a branch
creaking.

All night a boat swings as if to sink. Weight returning to weight in the
cold water. A hotel room returns from Wilmington into morning. A boat
sets out without boatmen into twenty years of snow returning.

THE STRUCTURE OF RIME XIII

Best of ways. That there be a law the Earth gives and the Mountain
stand over us, the Valley haunt us, the Shores between elements draw us.

Where is thy Jerusalem? Where is Chou perfected? land at the center? So that the stars arrange, named, into guardian orders.

The structure of rime is in the rigorous trees repeated that take on the swirl visible of the coast winds and the outcroppings, the upraised and bared granites that define sentences of force and instrument.

For the melted Earth has gone up out of the Sun into a law that is of stone. And light melodies of the sun—beauty that has shadows, great rests of dark-cast caverns in the living—play thereon.

For the first law, the stone tables of Moses or of Kung, are instruments of a light music, a melody from celestial orbs outswirld.

Aldebaran, El Nath, and the Raining Ones, the Pleiades, in the east, above the dark mountain. Eye, Horn and Heart of the Bull emerging.

And south, Lord over the dark water, the Scorpion entire, that from baleful Antares upreaches into the Scales of the Law. The rage of the heart ravishing or raising up. For the claws of the heart's bale are two points of the beam in Libra. For in french the fléau is a flail from which the scales hang that balance the soul created and its creation.

Best of ways. That there be a law under the stars. For the galaxies drift outward to enter a new universe.

That there be, where we are, a law. And, seeing the mountain, the stream defining the valley, the old sea, we say   *This*

is the place.

from *Roots and Branches* [1964]

ROOTS AND BRANCHES

     Sail, Monarchs, rising and falling
orange merchants in spring's flowery markets!
messengers of March in warm currents of news floating,
     flitting into areas of aroma,
tracing out of air unseen roots and branches of sense
     I share in thought,
filaments woven and broken where the world might light
     casual certainties of me. There are

     echoes of what I am in what you perform
this morning. How you perfect my spirit!
     almost restore
an imaginary tree of the living in all its doctrines
     by fluttering about,
intent and easy as you are, the profusion of you!
awakening transports of an inner view of things.

NEL MEZZO DEL CAMMIN DI NOSTRA VITA,

at 42, Simon Rodilla, tile-setter,
  "to do something big for America" began
the Watts towers
(this year, 1959, the officials of which city
 having initiated condemnation hearings
 against which masterpiece)

         three spires
   rising 104 feet, bejewelld with glass,
shells, fragments of tile, scavenged
   from the city dump, from sea-wrack,
taller than the Holy Roman Catholic church
   steeples, and, moreover,

inspired; built up from bits of beauty
　　sorted out—thirty-three years of it—
the great mitred structure rising
　　out of squalid suburbs where the
mind is beaten back to the traffic, ground
　　down to the drugstore, the mean regular houses
straggling out of downtown sections
　　of imagination defeated. "They're
taller than the Church," he told us
　　proudly.

Art, dedicated to itself!

The cathedral at Palma too
　　soard above church doctrine,
with art-nouveau windows and baldachine by Gaudí
　　gatherd its children
under one roof of the imagination.

The poem . . .

"The poet,"
Charles Olson writes,
"cannot afford to traffic in any other *sign* than his one"
"his self," he says, "the man
or woman he is" Who? Rodia
　　at 81 is through work.
Whatever man or woman he is,
　　he is a tower, three towers,
a trinity upraised by himself.
　　"Otherwise God does rush in."

Finisht.　"There are only his own
　　composed forms, and each one
the issue of the time of the moment of its creation,
not any ultimate except what he in his heat
and that instant in its solidity yield";

like the Tower of Jewels at the San Francisco
　　Panama-Pacific Exposition in 1915, this

"phantom kingdom to symbolize man's
   highest aims", glittering, but

an original, accretion of disregarded
   splendors
resurrected against the rules,
having in this its personal joke; its genius
   misfitting
the expected mediocre; an ecstasy
   of broken bottles
and colord dishes thrown up against whatever
   piety, city ordinance, plans,
risking height;

                    a fairy citadel,
a fabulous construction out of
   Christianity where Morgan le Fay
carries the King to her enchanted Isle
   —all glass beads of many colors
and rickety towers, concrete gardens,
   that imitate magnificence.

"Art," Burckhardt writes:
"the most arrogant traitor of all
putting eyes and ears . . . in place of
   profounder worship"
"substituting figures for feelings."

   The rounds contain crowns.
   The increases climb by bridges.

   The whole
planned to occupy life and allow
   for death:

                    a skeletal remain
as glory, a raised image, sceptre,
   spectral island, most arrogant,
"to do something big for America"

   Rodia.

APPREHENSIONS

1

To open Night's eye that sleeps in what we know by Day.
      "If the Earth were animate
it should not experience pleasure when grottoes and caves are dug
      out of its back"

From which argument my mind fell away
or disclosed a falling-away,
and I saw an excavation—but a cave-in of the ground,
hiding in showing, or showing in hiding,
a glass or stone, most valuable.

According to the text   ["Renaissance Cosmologies"
                                                by Paul-Henri Michel,
Ficino had the idea   *Diogenes,* 18]
      life circulates from the earth
      to the stars
"in order to constitute the uninterrupted
      tissue of the whole of nature."

You've to dig and come to see what I mean.
      Eidos, Idea,
"is something to which we gain access through sight."
This defines the borderlines of the meaning.
      For what I saw was only a gleam.
      I did not bring the matter to light.

Well, I saw . . . yes, that the earth is a great toad-mother,
      a fancy figure of Tiamat,
pitted with young. But then I stood
looking down into a chain of caves most real
(that might have been washt out, gutted
 by rains from the shit-yellow clay),

an opening archaeologists or a storm had dug
(at Qumrân fragments of an old way
      stored out of sight).

Michel remarks: *"Statements of this kind*
        are all the more valuable because they are rare"
        and *"Certain concordances reveal direct and more or less*
        disguised plagiarisms."

What I saw was only a gleam.
It might have been a living thing
for it moved in the muck.
I did not search it out.
The look was enough.

        (My mind had slipt again, could not
        keep its place in the sentence)
        "Whenever the subject is not the earth
        but the universe viewd as a whole"
           "divergences appear"

And the soul was reveald where it was,
fearful, rapt, prepared to withdraw
        from knowing,
looking down into the six-foot pit where . . .

Or it was a stone that is most rare,
        moving to see,
what we call a jewel, hidden there, formd
        in pressure and the inner fire.

        Ficino's text reads: *"How can one dare*
        to say that this woman's womb is not living
        since it produces little ones?"

2

THE DIRECTIVE

is a building. The architecture of the sentence
        allows
personal details,   portals
reverent and enchanting,
constructions from what lies at hand

                    to stand
for what rings true.
                         His concentration fixes this
                    island,
a space figured in language by where is placed
                    tower
and here bridge to the walls.

How they ploughd the given field in rows,
                    prose and
versus . and brought landscape
                    into being,

the grove interpreting and
          interpreted by the house and hearth—
                    a grave expectation

provides for the dome of many-colord glass,
                    jeweld light,
carved woods and deep windows;

needs hush of the high hall that from above
is deep, a well or wall of holy spirit
          defining the humble.

                    Where there is a temple
                    man's kept from base servitude.

     Let my awe be steady
in the rude elements of my household.
          At the window, the rose vine.

Sage Architect, you who awaken
the proportions and scales of the soul's wonder
     of stars and water,
               paeans of color
that bathe the cumulus at the horizon, yet
     direct
               discrete light
defining the lintel,

Bells tied in the foliage ring as the wind rises.

      *

I found a monument of what I am
around me as if waking were a dream,
a house built in the ancient time
when man like a salmon swam

in currents of fire and air, in what he was,
leapt to the ladders of desire
and read in the stream before there were letters
deep reflections of his cause.

There must be a pool, dark and steady mood,
stone and water, where this magic crossing,
this ray of a star, catches in flow
another time of what we always are,

from which we start up into the live jewel,
see joy hid where death most is,
ready like a seed encased in its shell.
O let the shadows and the light rays mix!

Sage Architect of the soul and its image,
let there be a household of these things
where such a silence awakens our fearful touch
and flames of beauty in old stuff rage.

I've to come into a loneliness, as if into a room
whose builder rememberd that Love stands alone
and workt in whose timbers a rude poetry
evoking the presence and weight of that crown.

The King brings his old body into its monument
in which we are rememberd, lonely and bare,
of one being, one presence,
slowly restoring the house of its kin.

The aged wood shines in the light,
surrounding and including the shine of our eyes.

Bells tied in the foliage
ring as the wind rises!

3

Dream or vision, the ancestors' adventure;
　　new food found in famine;
or manhood in the wounds of a woman's rage;
　　scooping the saintly skull
to eat of its virtue;
　　theft of fire; theft of what the heart desired
made so beautiful by theft's magic that
　　men still remember the walls of Troy,
the horse-traders' town; and young boys have heroic affinities,
　　immune by the Mother-Dragon's blood,
except that Eros marks one spot to be betrayd as His,
　　close upon Death.

All that we've lived obscured truth on these pages.

　　The elemental man is a humpt bank where
　　　　the hair grows, heapt up of time,
　　folded upon fold, lifted up from what he was,
　　　　a depth of silt, into this height
　　　　　　above sea level.

Compressions, oppressions—the horde gathering
　　in the poorest lands,
shifting the weight of continents. And continents
　　are only what giants must be.

Theosophists teach that primeval man is a vast dispersed being,
having as much intelligence in the sweep of his tail
as in his claws or those ravening jaws, back of whose
row on row of teeth ripping the meat
　　a brain like a child's fist pushing those eyes;

and see the force of intellectual hunger
　　focus, ravening towards such rest
a diamond has in structure, sustaind by pressure. Man

so exclusively defined he is
        a figure of light.

        Then hunger be stem
        from what I am,
and the hero bloom as he will toward that end
        the poem imitates by admitting a form.

To survive we conquer life or must find
dream or vision, the grandfathers' fathers' trail.
        But it was my grandfather who made that trek
after the war into the Oregon Territory
and my grandmother who enterd the dragon West
        enacting what is now a map
where we crawl on hands and knees along the edge of the rug
to the house of the Bear Chiefs
        in the blood-colord light and the purple light
            from her staind-glass window cast
        where by a river for a long time stayd
so that there is a continent of feeling beyond our feeling,
        a big house of the spirit,
indians and cowboys taking over the english-styled garden.
        Over and over: *"You're dead!"*
Only to jump up shouting, "This is play!"

This is play. They've come back from the wars.
        The German trophies shown on the balcony.
And the grown-ups discuss the death-throes
        of continents and civilizations.

        The tired old man
after that other war,
caught in the nets of marriage his wife wove
        taking to drink and whores
        as my grandfather did
—now that I know that story—
        but this is myth
that Freud says lies in our blood, Dragon-wise,
to darken our intelligence.

We remember it all.
The sinister children at table reject their food,
        spewing up bits,
member by member remember, part by part
        the cast, a bit in the play,
of the eyes, of the dice, of design toward crisis.

[reversion to First Movement]

They had taken him out of time.
He had taken them, parts of him,
out of what he was, left
detaild record of his form.

So that the earth
bereft of him
kept a crude resemblance.
The lowest room, at least,

stood for the head,
joind by a neck
to the trunk of the cave above.
It was not a grave then.

It was a place where a flood
had passionately dug out
his substance, leaving only his boundaries.
And it seemd a grave to me,

for I thought he was dead. No . .
it seemd a series of caves as I said.
Certainly, there were no arms or legs
clearly defined.

It did occur to me
that the hideous gleam of a crawling thing
        there at the bottom
was in the mind—
that the figure was head downwards.

I have seen the jewel.

To open Night's eye that sleeps in what we know by Day.

> In the grievous excavation he remains,
> as if an empty place waited

> body to my soul.

4 [STRUCTURE OF RIME XIV]

Cire perdue, waste that was wax to the edge melting, forecast I've known in every touch!   —thus the Lover addresst his unrest in the first uprising of the light that unspelld his surrounding dark: This night has so fingerd my soul that I awake a new, a workt figure of joy.

O play that Love makes out of Desire! What I was as a boy has run out and away so that I wept. Spectral images of manhood took shape in me.

I saw in your eyes—sudden, waiting, empty—a place I was to fill. As in the theater it can be shown, such a previousness to passion, a void

> prepared in its visible counter part—

song, *cire perdue,* river of me that flows away, melted from cast after cast, wax releasing fingerprint-fine intensions of the man from the world that is a worker in men. See! from Hesperus-Lucifer starts of light out of earliest thoughts toward me reach me, leaving scars of evening and morning,

> *cire perdue of love first known,*

lost wax that knew the shaping hand,

O cave of resemblances, cave of rimes!

5

(First Poem)

It is the earth turning
that lifts our shores from the dark
into the cold light of morning,
eastward turning,

and that returns us from the sun's burning
into passages of twilight and doubt,
dim reveries and gawdy effects.
The sun is the everlasting center of what we know,
a steady radiance.

The changes of light in which we dwell,
colors among colors that come and go,
are in the earth's turning.

Angels of light!   raptures of early morning!
your figures gather what they look like
out of what cells once knew of dawn,
first stages of love that in the water thrived.

So we think of sperm
as spark-fluid, many-milliond,
in light of the occult egg striking
doctrines.
          Twined angels of dark,
hornd master-reminders of from-where!
your snake- or animal-red eyes
store the fire's glare.

O flames! O reservoirs!

(Second Poem)

Handle the cards, shuffle the cards, cut and shuffle.
Distribute them once more upon the table.
Sometimes I am not permitted to read.

O I know the cards like an old poet knows his images,
but when I am not able to read they are only
numbers and faces, there are no moving pictures.

Cards of going, cards of coming . . .

These are not your cards or mine.
There is an angel of the time we are reading.
To figure his likeness men have ascribed

planetary governors, angels or gods, to the hours.
There is a god of the time where the cards fall.
You and I reading are meeting among his powers.

All things are powers within all things.
Think of the continuous presence
between the light of Venus or Mars and the eye

seeing the planet in the West in the evening
or the planet rising in the sign of Taurus near the Pleiades.
There is only one event.

There are old diagrams whose points are stars,
knots and associations that are men's gods,
or notes of a scale or possible scales to which music refers,

and think too of our speech where men
come again and again to their few words,
not of what they think they are saying

but of the thing they are telling, the mode
where they refer to the cards they are holding,
cards of going, cards of coming.

Numbers, letters, cards, words or hours
—handle and shuffle, cut and shuffle.
This one came before,

the image of grottoes or caves "dug out of the Earth's back"
arranged to suggest the cast of the Ancient of Days,
the Primordial Man.   Now it is gone.

It was in the distribution of words.

A worm or reflection of a star moved in
the depths. A star may be a crawling thing,
     as in the *old* deck,
something answers the moon or answers for the moon
     and changes movement.

Bruno of Nola saw such a universe.
     "In whatever region I am," he wrote,
*"time and place are distant mountains
changing their visages in the distant light."*

                    (Close)

March 27th: We found after the rains a cave-in along the path near the
rosemary and thyme, disclosing the pit of an abandond cess pool. Be-
cause of the dream fragment a month before, the event seems to have
been anticipated. A verification of the caves seen in actual life after they
had appeard in the life of the poem.

     Wherever we watch, concordances appear.

From the living apprehension, the given and giving *melos,*

     melodies thereof—in what scale?

Referring to these:

the orders of the sentence in reading;
the orders of what is seen in passing. There was the swarming earth;
the orders of commanding images;
the orders of passionate fictions and themes of the poet in writing;
the orders of the dead and the unborn that swarm in the floods of a
     man embracing his companion;
the orders of the Lord of Love. Let me await thee, Prince of the
     Morning;
the orders magnetic of the jewel that is secreted by the toads and coils
     of the brain;

the orders of the Architect building in the Likeness a temple;
the orders of the day that include the actual appearance of the pit
    in the garden;
the orders of stars and of words;

in these most marvelous.

    There is no life that does not rise
    melodic from scales of the marvelous.

To which our grief refers.

FOUR SONGS THE NIGHT NURSE SANG

    1

    How lovely all that glitters
    gold!

    "Day unto day uttereth speech,
    and night unto night
    sheweth knowledge"

    As in the old story
    at the shores of the sea
    the white swan is a maiden
    and sheds her clothes,

    the Moon sheds her light and returns.
    With her white story
    the wave breaks. See!

    This I lost I have found in you.
    Now I have seen fate with new eyes.

    O Swan, the lover has taken away
    your covering cast at the wave's edge.

    Dance on! Your arms
    embrace shadows, and you fling them out

into the sands, the years round you.
Your wings that were youth are gone!

The moon bathes nude in the cloud foam.
The black waters rush
into the light places.

2

It must be that hard to believe, for belief
must resist belief, pine-cone
that waits for death's fire to release its seed,
  —the Beast betrayd, forgotten,
at the edge of the pool dying, love withheld—
for the fire that destroys the living tree.

The Beast is the lord of the heart's need.
He must be hideous.
His is the Rose.
He is the First One.
Ask the Sun. Ask the Moon.
Go with the winds to the world's end.
He is beyond.

> *Come, my bride,*
> *Love has such need, He dies!*

The father's claim is what he fears. He warns her,
Do not return. He gives her
magic mirror, ring and glove
in trust. He tests her! *Tell no one*
your good fortune. Be on guard.
   My love is here.

It must be that hard to believe!
She must leave.

> *I have only a beast's heart,*
> *But O, return!*

Something must be lost, stolen.
Something must be told that should have been kept,

known by heart. He is all but forsworn.
Home could have won.

But the fate's turnd in the loss.
What was lockt
's released. *O*
most dear! the Beloved cries,
whose heart strains to answer the Beast's
enquiring eyes— *Love I am here!*

    Thou hast left the beast in need.
    At death's pool I lie.
    Now is the time to cry out
    against the human tree.

    "Seeing and hearing all things
    the eyes and ears of the great King waiting"
    I have been waiting to hear,
    I have been waiting to see,

seed in the burnt ground, past belief,
messenger come with news too late,
past the hour, past the bound,

        your voice that cries
Most dear!
        your searching eyes.

3

Madrone Tree that was my mother,
Cast me a cloak as red as your flower.
    My sisters don't know me,
    My father looks for me,
And I am by name the wind's brother.

Madrone Tree, from your thirsty root
feed my soul as if it were your fruit.
    Spread me a table and make it fair.
    Cast down splendor out of the air.
My story has only the wind's truth.

Madrone Tree, red as blood,
that once my mother was, be my rod.
Death came when I was born.
And from that earth now you are grown.
My father's a shadow, the wind is my god.

4

Let sleep take her, let sleep take her, let sleep
                    take her away!
The cold tears of her father
have made a hill of ice.
                    Let sleep take her.

Her mother's fear has made a feyrie.
                    Let sleep take her.
Now all of the kingdom lies down to die.
                    Let sleep take her.

Let dawn wake her, if dawn can find her.
        Let the prince of day take her
from sleep's dominion at the touch of his finger,
        if he can touch her.

The weather will hide her, the spider will bind her

            : so the wind sang.

O, there she lay
in an egg hanging from an invisible thread
spinning out I cannot tell whether

from a grave or a bed, from a grave or a bed.

STRUCTURE OF RIME XVI

                Back to the figure
of the man in the drill dancing.

His form enters the animal form. His stiff prick bears its head to the music. The makers of images scribble dancing limb upon dancing limb, phrase after phrase, horned head within horned head.

The voice dreaming within the bear skull said:

> *The bees have left the hives of my dream.*
> *The sun has not died, but in the rose of night and day*
> *the winged denizens of the light are gone,*
> *no longer to the seminal tip come,*
> *no longer to my naked bone.*

> *The honey is burnd into the rock.*
> *This I have seen where I went out.*
> *The bees have left the animal hive*
> *nor in the starry lanterns swarm.*

O my soul,
now man's desolation
    into his beginnings return!

STRUCTURE OF RIME XVII

This potion is love's portion. This herb
    her bliss.

        Helen among the wraiths
offerd this cup. Life's light in her eyes

    lit the lioness wrath.
In every part this mask is worn.

Climbing toward Its place in the sentence, the Word
    toward the sublime heard
Kundry laugh or came upon the edges
    of such a witch's smile.

He drank love from the maiden's lips.

There is nor crown nor cross   .
                    that does not reflect the serpent's scale
catching the sun's rays, the many faces   .
                    mirrord, the power and froth of the
sea's depths and shallows,
                    the masst glare.

This potion is love's portion. The heart of tomorrow's rose is today's sorrow
for tomorrow is gone. Yesterday has come into the song that Helen in the
sunlight sings:

> *This moment in my heart is crowded,*
> *masst with the glare of many kings.*
> *This hour is restless, masst with dead faces.*
> *This place falls away from its time.*
> *This rose falls away from its core.*
> *This cup falls away from my lover's hand and he shuts*
> *   his eyes.*
>
> *This herb is thistle, everlasting.*

Desire paces Eternity as if it had bounds, craving death.
The Word climbs upward into Its crown.

> Now for this time the lovers lie
> where Helen among the wraiths
> wreathes her spell.   Of thistles made.   *This herb*
>   *her bliss.*

OSIRIS AND SET

                    members of one Life Boat are
that rides against Chaos,
or into the night goes, driving back
      those darknesses within the dark,
as Harry Jacobus saw them on our mountain,
      trolls of the underground.

            Set lords it over them,
dark mind that drives before the dawn rays.

He is primitive terror, he is the prow,
he is first knowing
and, striving there, at the edge,
          has all of evil about him.

          Yes, he fought against Osiris,
conspired, scatterd the first light.
          He seduced the boy Horus, hawk-ghost of the sun,
to play the Hand to his cock.
He comes into the court of the law to remind us.
          He gives us the lie.

At one time our mother's brother, Set, was "Father"
          and taught us—what? ruining
our innocence. The great boat of the gods
          penetrates the thick meat,
sending quick nerves out that are tongues of light
          at the boundaries.   Foot, hand,
lips: a graph in *Scientific American,* September 1960,
          shows the design of sensory and motor intelligences.
We are so much mouth, mask, and hand,
          the hidden plan of volition can be read
                    (a secret that is presented to be seen
remaining secret) in the closed palm,
          in the human face.

          The radiant jewel of our own sun
held aloft by the dung beetle is the Child,
          our About-To-Be, Presence
in what's present.   There is nothing else.

          Feeling and motion, impression and expression,
                    contend. Drama
          is the shape of us. We are
                    ourselves tears and gestures of Isis
          as she searches for what we are ourselves,

          Osiris-Kadmon into many men shatterd,
                    torn by passion.   She-That-Is,
          our Mother, revives ever   His legend.

She remembers.   She puts it all together.
So that, in rapture, there is no longer
the sensory-motor homunculus
subduing the forces of nature, Horus contending with Set,

but the sistrum

sounds through us.

The Will wherein the gods ride

goes forward.

*

Hail! forgotten and witherd souls!

Our Mother comes with us   to gather her children!
Now it is time for Hell
to nurse at the teats of Heaven.

Dark sucks at the white milk.
Stars flow out into the deserted souls.

In our dreams we are drawn towards day once more.

AFTER READING H.D.'s *HERMETIC DEFINITIONS*

1

What time of day is it?
What day of the month?
H.D. read *quatrième* for *quantième*
in Perse. Today

the sky is overcast—dove's
(that may be her *nun's*) grey—
the light diffuse.

The light's everywhere diffused,
yet
we must take our direction
from the sun's quarter,

as if accurately, obey.
I cant remember, are the bees confused?
(I cant find the bee book
—the way books can get out of hand!)

They fly
by polarized light, take their way
in dance
making their map

as we likewise in song
keep time, but ("If you lose something,
you look *everywhere*—"
He is angry because I disturbd lunch

asking, Where is the bee book?
and could not figure out
—Would they lose their way,
the sun-track

under cloud-ceiling of grey,
the *quatrième*, as we might
lose the day of the month,
as if in song its key, not

know what moon in what season.

2

I do not remember
bees working over the garden on such a day.
But in the full sunlight
the warmth of its fire

hums;
and, coverd with pollens,

the honey gatherers
go to the heart of things,

shaking and waking the flowery horns,

taking the sweet of song
to fill their dark combs.

3

In the poem there is
"—*Are you dead in the darkness?*"
Who sleeps in the hive
where the Queen's honey is mixt?

Which they prepare
by what we call *instinct,*
as if they were sure,
nursing their own

Isis—"*générateur, générant*" the poem calls her
—drones and that other
Dreamer or Mother of them all
"who orderd, ordaind or controlld this"

the goddess or nurse commands
"*Write, write or die*".
We too write instinctively, like bees,
serve the Life of the Hive,

coverd with pollens out of time,
gold of the hour, tumble,
fly under maps of the sun's measure
on wings (words) that are winds

(melodies)
in the song's light
        stored
in the Queen's ward.

4

But the truth, he told me, was
he wasnt angry about lunch.
It was because
I hid what I wanted

from myself, made
the ease of the thing impossible;
teaching the mind
not to find the sun's rime;

setting the whole house into an uproar
—Is it *one*? Is it *tone*? Is it
imagination? What word are you
looking for?

(In a mimeographt "Lesson", of Dr. Quimby
On the Subconscious, I find
"He also calls it 'the book'
and he said

We are not any wiser than the book we have written")
where the bees came in,
came to mind, from *their* place or time
into this place, misplaced,

when I rememberd not where the book was
but their song in the sun.

FROM *THE MABINOGION*

To throw a window open
upon the marges of a sea!

In the closed room
when the party was going
we heard the ocean

out there.
      "Look out there!"
the old man warnd the young lords,
"Do not look out there.

"Yesterday is talking upon its sands.
Let it talk on. Do not

look out upon that land
for it is all water
    and washes the shores of this land away."

Do not look
away from this room of no remembrance.
Do not get up from this table,
these trophies, ennuies, celebrations.

Do not turn from this head of a great magic,
filld as it is with wars
and course of retribution after the wars.

To throw a window open!

Time is upon whose naked stretches

    hope roars

we saw the land behind us—

our wastes, our age, our hearts' loss
—and I do not know what we saw:

      this man a wreckt car,
      this man a Lover turn away,
      this man an empty glass upon the bar,
      this man a parody of what he was,
      because of our Lord.

      That is what the tale says.
      That is our adventure.

For I think we've been in
this joint before.

STRUCTURE OF RIME XX

The Master of Rime told me, You must learn to lose heart. I have
darkend this way and you yourself have darkend. Are you so blind you
cant see what you cant see?

You keep the unknown bird hidden in your hands as if to carry sight
into the house. But the sightless ones have opend the windows and listen
to the songs outside. *Absence*, the Mother of this Blindness tells them,
*rimes among the feathers of birds that exist only in sight. The songs you hear fall
from their flight light like shadows stars cast among you.*

You must learn to lose your heart. Let the beat of your heart go.
Missing the beat. And from the care of your folded hands unfold a
feeling in the room of an empty space. For the pit of despair wants you to
come there. The thrush waits trembling in the confinement of his mas-
ter's doubt and every bird among the watery eaves sings as his brother.

O brother of the confined! O my twin lord of the net rime has tied in
the tongues of fire.

And the Master of Rime appeard again, smiling. His hands cupt as
he went. His head bowd, looking down, seeking his way away from me.

BENDING THE BOW

We've our business to attend Day's duties,
bend back the bow in dreams as we may
til the end rimes in the taut string
with the sending. Reveries are rivers and flow
where the cold light gleams reflecting the window upon the
   surface of the table,
the presst-glass creamer, the pewter sugar bowl, the litter
   of coffee cups and saucers,
carnations painted growing upon whose surfaces. The whole
composition of surfaces leads into the other
              current disturbing
what I would take hold of. I'd been

in the course of a letter—I am still
in the course of a letter—to a friend,
who comes close in to my thought so that
the day is hers. My hand writing here
there shakes in the currents of . . . of air?
of an inner anticipation of . . . ? reaching to touch
ghostly exhilarations in the thought of her.

      At the extremity of this
         design
"there is a connexion working in both directions, as in
        the bow and the lyre"—
only in that swift fulfillment of the wish
        that sleep
      can illustrate my hand
       sweeps the string.

You stand behind the where-I-am.
The deep tones and shadows I will call a woman.
The quick high notes . . . You are a girl there too,

having something of sister and of wife,
            inconsolate,
and I would play Orpheus for you again,

            recall the arrow or song
            to the trembling daylight
            from which it sprang.

TRIBAL MEMORIES   **PASSAGES 1**

from the Emperor Julian, *Hymn to the Mother of the Gods:*

   And Attis encircles heavens like a tiara, and thence sets out as though to descend to
earth.
   •
   For the even is bounded, but the uneven is without bounds and there is no
way through or out of it.

And to Her-Without-Bounds I send,
wherever She wanders,   by what
        campfire at evening,

among tribes setting each the City where
            we Her people are
at the end of a day's reaches   here
        the Eternal
lamps lit, here   the wavering human
        sparks of heat and light
glimmer, go out, and reappear.

For this is the company of the living
and the poet's voice speaks from no
        crevice in the ground between
            mid-earth and underworld
breathing fumes of what is deadly to know,
            news larvae in tombs
            and twists of time do feed upon,

but from the hearth stone, the lamp light,
            the heart of the matter where the

                    house is held   •

yet here, the warning light at the edge of town!

The City will go out in time, will go out
            into time, hiding even its embers.
And we were scatterd thruout the countries and times of man

for we took alarm in ourselves,
                rumors of the enemy
spread among the feathers of the wing that coverd us.

•

Mnemosyne, they named her, the
                Mother with the whispering
            featherd wings.   Memory,
the great speckled bird who broods over the
                nest of souls, and her egg,
        the dream in which all things are living,
I return to, leaving my self.

I am beside myself with this
            thought of the One in the World-Egg,
enclosed,   in a shell of murmurings,

                rimed round,
                sound-chamberd child.

It's that first!   The forth-going to be
                bursts into green as the spring
            winds blow watery from the south
and the sun returns north.   He hides

            fire among words in his mouth

and comes racing out of the zone of dark and storm

towards us.

I sleep in the afternoon, retreating from work,
reading and dropping away from the reading,
as if I were only a seed of myself,
    unawakend,   unwilling
        to sleep or wake.

THE ARCHITECTURE   **PASSAGES 9**
                              6/6/64

". . . it must have recesses. There is a great charm in a room broken up
in plan, where that slight feeling of mystery is given to it which arises
when you cannot see the whole room from any one place . . when there
is always something around the corner"

from the window-shelter

the light

the curtains of daffodil-yellow

light
            beyond   •

a little night music

after   noon

• strains of *Mahagonny* on the phonograph

distant

intoxications of brazen crisis,

the (1930) *Können einem toten Mann nicht helfen* chorus

the procession with drum-roll

in the distance

recesst

(the stage becomes dark)

from the bookcases   the glimmering titles arrayd   keys
Hesiod   •   Heraklitus   •   *The Secret Books of the Egyptian Gnostics* . . .

"Take a house planned in this way, with a big living room, its great
fireplace, open staircase, casement windows, built-in seats, cupboards,
bookcases . . and perhaps French doors opening out upon a
porch" . . .

La *Révélation d'Hermès Trismégiste*
Plutarch's Morals: Theosophical Essays
Avicenna
The Zohar
The Aurora

I was reading while the music playd

curld up among the ornamental cushions

. . . "which links the house with the garden/ and

sparkling into the jeweld highlights given forth by
copper, brass, or embroideries"

"the staircase, instead of being hidden away in a small hall or treated as a
necessary evil, made one of the most beautiful and prominent features of
the room because it forms a link between the social part of the house and
the upper regions" . . .

Below the house   in the dark of the peppertree

stript to the moonlight   embraced

for the mystery's sake   mounting

thru us   •   the garden's recesses

"   'You are to make it,' I told you in the past.   I do not suppose you recognize me.   'Owl' is what I am calld.   This is how I am."

They saw an owl.

Phantastes, At the Back of the North Wind,
The Princess and the Goblin,
The Princess and Curdie,   Lilith

the lamplight   warm   upon the page where I   •

romance   •   in which lost, reading   •

"   You will often tell the story. If you do that you will be able to marry those you love. You will fear me. If I even see you, you will die."

. . . "which belong to the inner and individual part of the family life."

THE FIRE   **PASSAGES 13**

jump	stone	hand	leaf	shadow	sun
day	plash	coin	light	downstream	fish
first	loosen	under	boat	harbor	circle
old	earth	bronze	dark	wall	waver
new	smell	purl	close	wet	green
now	rise	foot	warm	hold	cool

blood   disk

horizon   flame

The day at the window

the rain at the window

the night and the star at the window

Do you know the old language?

I do not know the old language.

Do you know the language of the old belief?

From the wood we thought burning

our animal spirits flee,   seeking refuge wherever,

as if in Eden,   in this   panic

lion and lamb lie down,   quail

heed not the eagle in flight before the flames high

over head go.

We see at last the man-faced roe and his

gentle mate;   the wild boar too

turns a human face.   In whose visages no terror

but a philosophic sorrow shows.   The ox

is fierce with terror, his thick tongue

slavers and sticks out panting

to make the gorgoneion face.

(This is Piero di Cosimo's great painting *A Forest Fire*, dated 1490-1500, preserved in the Ashmolean Museum at Oxford)

He inherits the *sfumato* of Leonardo da Vinci—

there is a softening of outline,   his color fuses.

A glow at the old borders makes

magic Pletho, Ficino, Pico della Mirandola prepared,

reviving in David's song,

Saul in his flaming rage heard,   music

Orpheus first playd,

chords and melodies of the spell that binds

the many in conflict in contrasts of one mind:

"For, since song and sound arise from the cognition of the mind, and the impetus of the phantasy, and the feeling of the heart, and, together with the air they have broken up and temperd, strike the aerial spirit of the hearer, which is the junction of the soul and the body, they easily move the phantasy, affect the heart and penetrate into the deep recesses of the mind"

Di Cosimo's   featherd, furrd, leafy

boundaries where   even the Furies are birds

and blur   in higher harmonies Eumenides;

whose animals, entering a charmd field

in the light of his vision, a stillness,

have their dreamy glades and pastures.

The flames, the smoke.   The curious

sharp focus in a glow   sight

in the Anima Mundi has.

Where in the North (1500) shown in Bosch's illumination:

Hell breaks out   an opposing music.

The faces of the deluded   leer, faint, in lewd praise,

close their eyes in voluptuous torment,

enthralld by fear,   avidly

following the daily news: the earthquakes, eruptions,
flaming automobiles, enraged lovers, wars against communism,
heroin addicts, police raids, race riots . . .

caught in the *lascivia animi* of this vain sound.

And we see at last the faces of evil openly

over us,

bestial extrusions no true animal face knows.

There are rats, snakes, toads, Boehme tells us,

that are the Devil's creatures.   There is

a Devil's mimic of man, a Devil's chemistry.

The Christ closes His eyes,   bearing the Cross

as if dreaming.   Is His Kingdom

not of this world, but a dream of the Anima Mundi,

the World-Ensouling?

The painter's *sfumato* gives His face

pastoral stillness amidst terror,   sorrow

that has an echo in the stag's face we saw before.

About Him, as if to drown   sweet music out,

                  Satan looks forth from
men's faces:
                  Eisenhower's idiot grin, Nixon's
black jaw, the sly glare in Goldwater's eye, or
the look of Stevenson lying in the U.N. that our
Nation save face   •

His face multiplies from the time of Roosevelt, Stalin,
Churchill, Hitler, Mussolini;   from the dream
of Oppenheimer, Fermi, Teller, Vannevar Bush,

brooding the nightmare formulae—to win the war!   the

inevitable   •   at Los Alamos

plotting the holocaust of Hiroshima   •

Teller openly for the Anti-Christ

•   glints of the evil that one sees in the power of this world,

"In the North and East, swarms of dough-faces, office-vermin, kept
editors, clerks, attaches of ten thousand officers and their parties,
aware of nothing further than the drip and spoil of politics—
ignorant of principles . . . In the South, no end of blusterers,
braggarts, windy, melodramatic, continually screaming, in falsetto, a
nuisance to These States, their own just as much as any . . . and
with the most incredible successes, having pistol'd, bludgeoned,
yelled and threatend America, these past twenty years, into one long
train of cowardly concessions, and still not through but rather at the
commencement. Their cherished secret scheme is to dissolve the
union of These States . . ."
                                            (Whitman, 1856)

faces of Princes, Popes, Prime Usurers, Presidents,
Gang Leaders of whatever Clubs, Nations, Legions   meet

to conspire, to coerce, to cut down   •

Now, the City, impoverisht, swollen, dreams again

the great plagues—typhus, syphilis, the black buboes

epidemics,   manias.

My name is Legion   and in every nation   I multiply.

Over those who would be Great Nations   Great Evils.

They are burning the woods, the brushlands, the

grassy fields razed;   their

profitable suburbs spread.

Pan's land, the pagan countryside, they'd

lay waste.

cool	green	waver	circle	fish	sun
hold	wet	wall	harbor	downstream	shadow
warm	close	dark	boat	light	leaf
foot	purl	bronze	under	coin	hand
rise	smell	earth	loosen	plash	stone
now	new	old	first	day	jump

MY MOTHER WOULD BE A FALCONRESS

My mother would be a falconress,
And I, her gay falcon treading her wrist,
would fly to bring back
from the blue of the sky to her, bleeding, a prize,
where I dream in my little hood with many bells
jangling when I'd turn my head.

My mother would be a falconress,
and she sends me as far as her will goes.
She lets me ride to the end of her curb
where I fall back in anguish.
I dread that she will cast me away,
for I fall, I mis-take, I fail in her mission.

She would bring down the little birds.
And I would bring down the little birds.
When will she let me bring down the little birds,
pierced from their flight with their necks broken,
their heads like flowers limp from the stem?

I tread my mother's wrist and would draw blood.
Behind the little hood my eyes are hooded.
I have gone back into my hooded silence,
talking to myself and dropping off to sleep.

For she has muffled my dreams in the hood she has made me,
sewn round with bells, jangling when I move.
She rides with her little falcon upon her wrist.
She uses a barb that brings me to cower.
She sends me abroad to try my wings
and I come back to her. I would bring down
the little birds to her
I may not tear into, I must bring back perfectly.

I tear at her wrist with my beak to draw blood,
and her eye holds me, anguisht, terrifying.
She draws a limit to my flight.
Never beyond my sight, she says.

She trains me to fetch and to limit myself in fetching.
She rewards me with meat for my dinner.
But I must never eat what she sends me to bring her.

Yet it would have been beautiful, if she would have carried me,
always, in a little hood with the bells ringing,
at her wrist, and her riding
to the great falcon hunt, and me
flying up to the curb of my heart from her heart
to bring down the skylark from the blue to her feet,
straining, and then released for the flight.

My mother would be a falconress,
and I her gerfalcon, raised at her will,
from her wrist sent flying, as if I were her own
pride, as if her pride
knew no limits, as if her mind
sought in me flight beyond the horizon.

Ah, but high, high in the air I flew.
And far, far beyond the curb of her will,
were the blue hills where the falcons nest.
And then I saw west to the dying sun—
it seemd my human soul went down in flames.

I tore at her wrist, at the hold she had for me,
until the blood ran hot and I heard her cry out,
far, far beyond the curb of her will   •

to horizons of stars beyond the ringing hills of the world where
    the falcons nest
I saw, and I tore at her wrist with my savage beak.
I flew, as if sight flew from the anguish in her eye beyond her sight,
sent from my striking loose, from the cruel strike at her wrist,
striking out from the blood to be free of her.

My mother would be a falconress,
and even now, years after this,
when the wounds I left her had surely heald,
and the woman is dead,

her fierce eyes closed, and if her heart
were broken, it is stilld   •

I would be a falcon and go free.
I tread her wrist and wear the hood,
talking to myself, and would draw blood.

THE TORSO   **PASSAGES 18**

Most beautiful!   the red-flowering eucalyptus,
the madrone, the yew

Is he . . .

So thou wouldst smile, and take me in thine arms
The sight of London to my exiled eyes
Is as Elysium to a new-come soul

If he be Truth
I would dwell in the illusion of him

His hands unlocking from chambers of my male body

such an idea in man's image

rising tides that sweep me towards him

. . . *homosexual?*

and at the treasure of his mouth

pour forth my soul

his soul   commingling

I thought a Being more than vast, His body leading
into Paradise,   his eyes

quickening a fire in me,   a trembling

hieroglyph: At the root of the neck

the clavicle, for the neck is the stem of the great artery
upward into his head that is beautiful

At the rise of the pectoral muscle,

the nipples, for the breasts are like sleeping fountains
of feeling in man, waiting above the beat of his heart,
shielding the rise and fall of his breath, to be
awakend

At the axis of his mid hriff

the navel, for in the pit of his stomach the chord from
which first he was fed has its temple

At the root of the groin

the pubic hair, for the torso is the stem in which the man
flowers forth and leads to the stamen of flesh in which
his seed rises

a wave of need and desire over   taking me

cried out my name

(This was long ago.   It was another life)

and said,

What do you want of me?

I do not know, I said.   I have fallen in love.   He
has brought me into heights and depths my heart
would fear   without him.   His look

pierces my side   •   fire eyes   •

I have been waiting for you, he said:
                    I know what you desire

        you do not yet know   but through me   •

    And I am with you everywhere.   In your falling

I have fallen from a high place.   I have raised myself

            from darkness in your   rising

                    wherever you are

        my hand in your hand   seeking   the locks, the keys

I am there.   Gathering me, you gather

        your Self   •

    For my Other is not a woman but a man

    the King upon whose bosom let me lie.

UP RISING   **PASSAGES 25**

Now Johnson would go up to join the great simulacra of men,
        Hitler and Stalin, to work his fame
        with planes roaring out from Guam over Asia,
all America become a sea of toiling men
        stirrd at his will, which would be a bloated thing,
        drawing from the underbelly of the nation
        such blood and dreams as swell the idiot psyche
        out of its courses into an elemental thing
        until his name stinks with burning meat and heapt honors

And men wake to see that they are used like things
        spent in a great potlach, this Texas barbecue
            of Asia, Africa, and all the Americas,

And the professional military behind him, thinking
    to use him as they thought to use Hitler
    without losing control of their business of war,

But the mania, the ravening eagle of America
    as Lawrence saw him "bird of men that are masters,
    lifting the rabbit-blood of the myriads up into . . . "
    into something terrible, gone beyond bounds, or
As Blake saw America in figures of fire and blood raging,
    . . . in what image? the ominous roar in the air,
the omnipotent wings, the all-American boy in the cockpit
    loosing his flow of napalm, below in the jungles
    "any life at all or sign of life" his target, drawing now
        not with crayons in his secret room
the burning of homes and the torture of mothers and fathers and
    children,
    their hair a-flame, screaming in agony, but
in the line of duty, for the might and enduring fame
    of Johnson, for the victory of American will over its victims,
    releasing his store of destruction over the enemy,
in terror and hatred of all communal things, of communion,
    of communism •

has raised from the private rooms of small-town bosses and business-
    men,
from the council chambers of the gangs that run the great cities,
    swollen with the votes of millions,
from the fearful hearts of good people in the suburbs turning the
    savory meat over the charcoal burners and heaping their barbecue
    plates with more than they can eat,
from the closed meeting-rooms of regents of universities and sessions
    of profiteers

—back of the scene: the atomic stockpile; the vials of synthesized
    diseases eager biologists have develops over half a century dreaming
    of the bodies of mothers and fathers and children and hated rivals
    swollen with new plagues, measles grown enormous, influenzas
    perfected; and the gasses of despair, confusion of the senses, mania,
    inducing terror of the universe, coma, existential wounds, that
    chemists we have met at cocktail parties, passt daily and with a

happy "Good Day" on the way to classes or work, have workt to
make war too terrible for men to wage—

raised this secret entity of America's hatred of Europe, of Africa, of
    Asia,
the deep hatred for the old world that had driven generations of
    America out of itself,
and for the alien world, the new world about him, that might have
    been Paradise
but was before his eyes already cleard back in a holocaust of burning
    Indians, trees and grasslands,
reduced to his real estate, his projects of exploitation and profitable
wastes,

this specter that in the beginning Adams and Jefferson feard and knew
would corrupt the very body of the nation
    and all our sense of our common humanity,
this black bile of old evils arisen anew,
takes over the vanity of Johnson;
and the very glint of Satan's eyes from the pit of the hell of
    America's unacknowledged, unrepented crimes that I saw in
    Goldwater's eyes
now shines from the eyes of the President
    in the swollen head of the nation.

STAGE DIRECTIONS   **PASSAGES 30**

> *"It's not so, not strictly so,*
>   *that's the trouble,"* Ezra Pound, Venice
> 1964

Slowly the toiling images will rise,
Shake off, as if it were débris,
    the unnecessary pleasures of our lives
And all times and intents of peaceful men
Reduce to an interim, a passing play,
    between surpassing
Crises of war.
                    Upon the stage before:

He brings the camera in upon the gaping neck
   which now is an eye of bloody meat   glaring
   from the womb of whose pupil   sight

springs to see,   two   children of adversity.

The Mother's baleful glance in romance's
                        head of writhing snakes haird

      freezes the ground.

                Okeanos   roars,

wild oceanic father,   visage   compounded of fury and of wind

  (the whole poem becoming a storm   in which faces arise)

     Mouths yawn immensely   and hours,
                    as if they were mad brothers,
stare.

       From the body of the poem, all that words create
  presses forth to be: youth,   with lightning flash
   that now is sword of gold, two-edged,
              or of sun-glare
  cutting eye-nerve,
        painful youth!

   And Pegasos springs   "born near the *springs* of Ocean"

     ὸτ Ὠκεανου περι πηγας γενθ

He-who-spurts-up   from the broken arteries   carotids   out of

   deep sleep the blood carries   upward

        (Ocean then, the drowsy deep)

   awakend

flies

to Zeus-Father above,
                    Lord of the Deep Skies, whose House
          awaits him,
                    the pressure of whose tides

upon the shores of life is like a horse raging,
          thunderous hooves,   striking

                    flashes of light from unbright matter.

In the carved panel of the sarcophagus from Golgoi
[The Metropolitan Museum of Art, *Handbook of
the Cesnola Collection of Antiquities from Cyprus.*
As given in Cook, *Zeus,* volume two, part one, page
718]

the twain   rise to form for this moment
     the head of a new monster

                         Genius

so starts up, affrighted,   of sudden stroke

     "the which a double nature has" (Spenser

          telling his syllables here)

that from the Garden verse addresses   each word

               "It sited was in fruitfull soyle of old,
               "And girt in with two walles on either side;
               "The one of yron, the other of bright gold,
               "That none might thorough breake, nor ouer-stride:
               "And double gates it had, which opened wide"

               the wound become so wide a door
a deed
          (the skull fragments and brain splatterd over the car's
          upholstery,   the red of blood and roses mixing

in a flash)

(*"So foule and faire a day I have not seene,"* another
murderous heart declares, who from Medusa's head
expects that Burning Would—to echo Joyce's pun—
will never come to Dance Inane:

> *"Come, seeling Night,*
> *"Skarfe up the tender Eye of pitiful Day,"* he cries:
> *"And with thy bloodie and invisible Hand*
> *"Cancell and teare to pieces that great Bond,*
> *"Which keepes me pale.   Light thickens . . ."*

Shakespeare sees how in the assassin's mind
the world is filld with enemies,   the truth
itself is enemy and quickens   action to override
subversive thought.

> *"Ile fight,"* Macbeth declares: *"Give me my Armor."*

> *"Tis not needed yet."*

> *"Ile put it on:*
> *"Send out more Horses; skirre the Country round,*
> *"Hang those that talke of Feare . . ."*)

in which the nation's secreted
sum of evil is betrayd

> Dionysos, Zeus's Second Self,

> Director of the Drama,
> needed.

*

Dark figures move, flares / scatter in the night.
And from the stage / wild hammerings, a frightful pulse
Begins. Behind the lids / an after-image burns
And the tortured spirit in the meat remembers now
The nation has gone so far in wrong / Truth grows fateful
And true song gives forth portents of woe.   Sublime

Forbidden intensities convert the personal,
        and from what *I* am
Masks of an old pageant, from my world and time
Portentous rimes, foreshadowings history become a plot demands.
        The dramatist
Would not misunderstand the *melos* "romantic and sensational,
        with both song and instrumental music interspersed"
Taking over the place of the Real, dims humanity and moves us
        toward its own End.   *Melodramatic*

His language, and from his troubled mind
Echoes of speeches, incantations, wild prayers,
As if to teach us "the perfection of certain ideals,
        the depravity of others", he casts upon the wind.

            (The President
                orders history
                reupholsterd)

Upon the sarcophagus of we know not whom,
each figure, impending, become a sign,

            Perseus with the head in a wallet
            turns his back and marches off
            ("to be followd by his hound," the scholar observes
            —exactly the figure of Le Mat in the
            Ancien Tarot de Marseilles—"hounded" then).
            Another figure gives Perseus wingd cap,
            sandals and caduceus of Hermes: Macbeth
            so little knows he moves as
            messenger of the myth, the
                plot of the play.

And from the dying body of America I see,
or from my dying body,
                            emerge

        children of a deed long before this deed,
        seed of Poseidon, depth in which the blue above
        is reflected

       released

huge Chrysaor and Pegasos   sword and flash

      Father of Geryon,   of him
        who carries Dante and Virgil into Hell's depths,

      and Steed of Bellerophon

        beneath whose hooves   once again
        new springs are loosed on Helicon.

from *Ground Work: Before the War* [1984]

ACHILLES' SONG

I do not know more than the Sea tells me,
told me long ago,   or I overheard Her
    telling distant roar upon the sands,
waves of meaning in the cradle of whose
    sounding and resounding power I
slept.

Manchild, She sang

—or was it a storm uplifting the night
    into a moving wall in which
I was carried as if a mothering nest had
    been made in dread?

the wave of a life darker than my
    life before me sped,   and I,
larger than I was,   grown dark as
    the shoreless depth,
arose from myself,   shaking the last
    light of the sun
from me.

Manchild,   She said,

Come back to the shores of what you are.
Come back to the crumbling shores.

All night
the mothering tides in which your
    life first formd in the brooding
light   have quencht the bloody
    splendors of the sun

and, under the triumphant processions
    of the moon,   lay down
thunder upon thunder of an old
    longing,   the beat

of whose repeated spell
    consumes you.

                    Thetis, then,
        my mother, has promised me
the mirage of a boat,   a vehicle
    of water within the water,
and my soul would return from
    the trials of its human state,
from the long siege,   from the
    struggling companions upon the plain,
from the burning towers and deeds
    of honor and dishonor,
the deeper unsatisfied war beneath
    and behind the declared war,
and the rubble of beautiful,   patiently
    workt   moonstones, agates, jades, obsidians,

turnd and returnd in the wash of
    the tides,   the gleaming waste,
    the pathetic wonder,

words turnd in the phrases of song
    before our song . . . or are they

beautiful,   patiently workt   remembrances of those
    long gone from me,
returnd anew,   ghostly in the light
    of the moon,   old faces?

For Thetis, my mother, has promised
    me a boat,
a lover,   an up-lifter of my spirit
    into the rage of my first element

rising,   a princedom
    in the unreal,   a share in Death.

*

Time, time.   It's time.

The business of Troy has long been done.

Achilles in Leuke has come home.

And soon you too   will be alone.

                        —December 10, 1968

[NOTE: In our Anglo-American convention we would pronounce the
diphthong in *Leuke* to foreshadow the rime in the word *you*—but in my
hearing of the line, remembering the voice of H.D.'s reading from her
Helen in Egypt, the name *Leuke* came to me sounded as in the German
convention to echo the diphthong in *Troy*.]

THE CONCERT   **PASSAGES 31**

Out of the sun and the dispersing stars
    go forth the elemental sparks,
    outpouring vitalities,
stir in the *Salitter* of the earth
    a *living* Spirit,
and the stars, mothers of light, remain,
    having each
its own "organic decorum, the complete
loyalty of a work of art to a shaping
    principle
            within itself"—

        that lonely spirit

having in its derivation likewise
the quality of the stars and yet

a severd *distinct* thing;   and the stars also
    are and remain   severe and distinct,
        each being of the universe   free to itself
            having its own law.

Yet the quality of the stars
reigneth in the spirit;   tho the spirit can
and may raise or drown itself
        in its own qualities,   or take its life
in the influence of the stars,   as it pleaseth.
        For it is free.   It has got for its own
the qualities it has in itself,   its own

        plot or myth,   its feel
        of what   belongs to it

                        —thus Boehme
    in his *Aurora or Morning Redness in the
        Rising of the Sun.*

First there is the power, and in the power
        is the tone or tune,
so that all of creation moves with
        a music,   the sound having its open
doors in the mind;   but in the heart
        lieth its fountain
            (as it doth also in Man).
        The second is *Mercurius.*   The musician

        has wound up his pegs
and tuned his strings.   He bends his head
        to hear the sound he makes
        that leads his heart upward,

ascending to where the beat breaks
     into an all-but-unbearable whirling crown
of feet dancing,   and now he sings   or it is
     the light singing,   the voice
shaking,   in the throes of the coming melody,
     resonances of meaning exceeding what we
understand,   words freed from their origins,

     obedient to tongues (sparks) (burning)
speech-flames   outreaching the heart's measure.

     It is the Star Betelgeuse, Alpha Orionis,
pouring its light within the depths,
          a single note its sphere,   each
"word"   a severd distinct thing,   Eternity
     already gone up into "MUST   MUST   MUST"
the Poet,   his heart urgent,
     leaping beyond him, writes: "MOVE,
INSTANTER, ON ANOTHER!"   "Prophecy,

which uncovers the mystery of future events
but which also reveals what lurks in the heart
—prayers . . . song and especially ecstatic
     speaking in tongues"

They shout,   leaping upon the tables,
     outpouring vitalities,   stammering—

"Doubtless," the scholar remarks,
     "the content of such enthusiastic utterances,
     except where they are completely unintelligible,
     is always assumed to be appropriate,
but that is not what makes them *spiritual gifts*—"

     the isolated satyr each man is,
severd distinct thing,   taking his word,
     his "mouth", his own, there, at the gate
or door   the sound forces in the mind

from the heart-spring.

                              I saw

willingly the strain of my heart break
    and pour its blood thundering at the life-locks

to release   full   my man's share of the stars'

        majesty   thwarted.

BEFORE THE JUDGMENT   **PASSAGES 35**

    Discontent with that first draft.   Where one's own
        hatred enters   Hell   gets out of hand.

    Again and again   Virgil   ever standing by Dante
        must caution him.   In Malebolge

    where the deep violation begins,

        Mentr' io laggiù fissamente mirava,
        lo duca mio, dicendo   "Guarda, guarda"

and here,   wrapt in the stench of vegetable rot,

        destroyd forests and fields,
                and from the villages   the putrid dead,
        phantasms of industrial enterprise
            swell fat upon the news of the daily body-count;

    after the age of lead, the age of gas,   fossil fuels
        oil slick on the water,   petroleum spread,
            the stink of gasoline in the murky air,
        the smoking tankers crawl towards Asia—

    men with fossil minds,   with oily tongues
        "to lick the mirror of Narkissos,"

oil slick over the pool there . . .

where not only that first face saw but how many others
work in the industries of *this* Hell,

betrayers of public trust   —under Johnson,
monetary expansion   to finance the War
the modern form of "printing press" money—

but their deals and names   sink into the mire,

new faces and souls to work new damnations
rise to the surface

quando il maestro mi disse   "Or pur mira!
che per poco è che teco non mi risso"

Dante being so drawn into a fascination by the controversies of the place

"And as one who dreams of something hurtful to him," he tells us—
"and dreaming   wishes it were a dream
so that he longs for that which is,   as if it were not"

Again his words come into ours   and Virgil's words would draw me back

into the orders of his art.

[Brought into English prose by John Aitkin Carlyle, 1849,
revised in 1867,   of whom his brother Thomas Carlyle wrote
"I wish him to be regarded as my second self, my surviving self"
—the text then belonging to the Mystery of these Passages—

for after Carlyle's *"The Hero as Poet: Dante, Shakespeare"*
Ezra Pound's *Spirit of Romance* opens our own period with his
announcement that *"The study of literature is hero-worship"*

Poetry having also its liturgy]

For they go about everywhere over the earth,

attendants,   daimons not only of men but of earth's plenitudes,
ancestral spirits of whatever good we know,

   wherever judgment is made they gather round watching,
   what the heart secretly knows they know,

clothed in mist, golden, ever existing, the host that comes in to
                 [conscience,

   deathless they swarm in Memory and feed at the honey-
                   [comb.

  τοὶ μὲν δαίμονες ἁγνοὶ Hesiod tells us they are
             [calld these

   truly *full of awe* holy unstaind by bloodshed

ἐπιχθόνιοι spirits of earth καλέονται they are named.

   We call them by name. The Master of Rime is among
                   [them.

And She whose breast is in language the Overwhelming

sends her own priestesses of the Boundless to these councils of our
                 [boundaries,

  divine women of that generation, shores and islands their
                 [precincts.

   And that there are islands in Time,

     and even in War, and in the Time of Retribution

         (his Hell our common-
                [wealth)

    they return to us,

  ἐσθλοί abounding, Mind returning, a Child, to the
                [Goods of Intellect

as if to his Paradise, a secret state of Mind we obey,
shaking the powers of this state from within.

Each actual moment   a seed,

where Love enters   the Milk-Light flows from the Center.

The Golden Ones move in invisible realms,
wrapt round in our thought as in a mist,

and the forces of Speech give way to the Language beyond Speech,

the Sea the sea reminds us of,
the Hosts of the Word that attend our words,

even in the surge of recognition our own grasp faltering
we can barely read,   we are unsure   even of the mean-
[ing that haunts us,
—it is all Greek to us—   having what ground here?

unsteadily,

slowly, piecing out this passage of Hesiod that has long lingerd at the
[threshold of the poem,

evoking from the steady clear flame that drew us   its secret

and from the ancestors of the household we keep   even in
[adversity

their voice   my voice   we come upon the fire   hidden,
[smouldering

we thought lost beyond reach . . .

Can you give me a light?

(He leans forward in the dark of yearning   fearfully
[unprepared)

In the shed there is only a smoky lantern   we work by.
The cows stir in their stanchions.
                        We kept the old rituals only one season.

And if you have ever kept my orders   I shall stand by you.

And Virgil to Dante: "Even now your thoughts have enterd into
                                                    [mine,

        with similar act and similar face;   so that

            of both I have made one resolve."

    So there was a covenant made with Good and into its orders I was
                                                    [born.
    There was a covenant made that we call the Age of Gold, the An-
                                            [cestral Design,
        and this alone governs what endures.

    And I was immersed into the depths of the Water,
        let down by that man who stood for my Father
        into the Element before Intention

    (or, in another version, cast into the Flood
        drownd in the rage of the Mother of What Is).

    I am speaking now of the Dream in which America sleeps, the New
                                                    [World,
    moaning, floundering, in three hundred years of invasions, our own
                                                    [history

        out of Europe and enslaved Africa.
    Tears stream down to feed the Deeps below
    from those eyes in which the spirits of America's yearning
    come and go, broken, reassembling, enduring, defeated . . .

    And will there be men to come who will remember
    the names of the presidents, governors, mayors
            this profound Evil has placed over us,
    each appropriate to his circle of the Inferno?

the powers of business and industry taking over government
    —War, the biggest business of all—
the interests of property the ultimate basis of this order?

They gave us the business.   And Congress divided,
but the majority again and again for self-interest and profit
and to make good the Lie
    against the well-being of the people,

armies abroad and spies in every nation,   false witnesses,
and at home the cops in the street now,   "the law"   supplanting the
                                                        [Law,
    having full mandate from the courts to kill without question,

back of the scene the bosses and war-mongers, misusers of the
                                                        [public trust,

    heads of the Hydra that Pound named *Usura,*

remember this time   for it returns   this betrayal of what we
                                                        [are
        among the people likewise   armd camps arise, and
                agents provocateurs keep the sources of trouble alive

    —in his Hell Cantos   he named it

    "the slough of unamiable liars,
            bog of stupidities,
    malevolent stupidities, and stupidities"

        —we've got it   with new faces.

    In the highest   this hatred

doing away with public services as the cost of the government's self
                                                        [service rises,
    in every domain fighting to destroy the humanities,

        in the lowest   as if it streamd out from the governing centers destroyers of cities and orders

. . . their public faces, names . . . Rubin, Hayakawa, Alioto, Reagan,
                                                                        [Nixon
    as we go upward the stupidity thickens,

    reflections in the oil slick multiplied.

    The Hydra prepares in every domain,   even in the revolution,

        his offices.

    His clowns come forward to entertain us.

And will there be men who will remember

the Devil's legions had their votes, ward-workers, enthusiasts, willing
agents?   And there came the amateurs of Hell,   the volunteer demons
        hungry for the look of fear their eyes would
feed upon,   men devourd by hatred devouring hatred.   And certain
                                                                        [tribes
    shouting their own outrages against Man's nature

            in that place   at Malebolge

        Alla man destra vidi nuova pietà,
        nuovi tormenti e nuovi frustatori,

            in every party   partisans of the torment.

            Tyranny throws up from its populace a thousand
            tyrant faces,   seethes and dies down,   would-be
            administrators of the evil or challengers of the
                                                        [establishment
            seeking their share of the Power that eats us.

        Se le fazion che porti non son false . . .

            But whose face is this face?   so many
            having only Hell's loan of a face at interest—

he was but one of the many frogs croaking
from the desolate marsh,   seething,   collapsing,
that they call the Law,   figments of the media
                                    [surrounding them.

Is *that* a name?   Alioto?   There are a million
Opportunity, without generation, spews forth like
                                                [him
          to take over our cities.

This Slough extends thruout the Time of Man.

And from that wretchedness   he leans forth,

            fearfully,   as ever,   yearning . . .

    "In this mirror,"   the Angel replies,   *"our Councils darken."*

The president turns in his sleep and into his stupidity seep the images of
                                                [burning peoples.
The poet turns in his sleep,   the cries of the tortured and of those whose
                                                [pain

    survives after the burning   survive with him,   for continually
    he returns to early dreams of just retributions and reprisals inflicted
                                                [for his injuries.
The soldier gloating over and blighted by the burning bodies of children,
                                                [women and old men,
    turns in his sleep of Viet Nam or,
dreamless, inert, having done only his duty, hangs at the edge of such a
                                                [conscience to sleep.
The protestant turns in his sleep, setting fire to hated images,
    entering a deeper war against the war.   A deeper stupidity gathers.

The Golden Ones, the ancestors of our Good, cloak themselves in Sleep's
                                                [depth,
          eternally watching.

As if from the depths of Hell, the sleepers seek rest in what they are,
so that again   the Wish of Death lifts them
                          and passes over them.
                                              This pain you take
      is the pain in which Truth turns like a key.

This Confession that struggles within you   and grows,
this *History of My True Country*   that you have come to acknowledge,
will not let you alone.   And the Eternal Ones of the Dream
cast you forth from them.

                  The Guardian moves as I am moved.

It is like a movement perceived in a stone.   Beyond my will,
unwilling,   I am moved.
                        The Jews use the name *Israel,*
you use the name *America*   or the name *Man,*   as if for a chosen
                                                          [tribe
or nation or for one animal species   the Grand Design labord,
            or for the Orders of Life labord,

but the Golden Ones meet in the Solar Councils
and their alphabet is hidden in the evolution of chemical codes.

            In this place the airy spirit
            catching fire in its fall from flight
            has started a burning of conscience
            in the depths of earth and the primal waters,
            and all of Creation rises to meet him,

            as if to answer a call,   as if to call   into Being,
            forth from a raging Absence, even among men,
            the Body of "Man" cries out   toward Him.

Children of Kronos,   of the Dream beyond death,

      secret of a Life   beyond our lives,

      having their perfection   as we have,

their bodies a like grace, a music,   their minds a joy, abundant,

    foliate,   fanciful in its flowering,

come into these orders as they have ever come,   stand,

    as ever,   where they are acknowledged,

against the works of unworthy men, unfeeling judgments, and cruel
                                                        [deeds.

BRING IT UP FROM THE DARK

Bring up from the dark water.
It will be news from behind the horizon.
Refugees, nameless people.   Who are they?
What is happening?   I do not know.
Out there.   Where we can see nothing.
Where we can do nothing.   Men of our own country
send deadly messengers we would not send.
The cold wind of their desolation chills the first hint of morning,
rumors of burnd houses, smoking fields, and now wraiths
of the dead men daily they kill rise
against us.   It will go against us,
    pass, sweep on and beyond us.

The great house of our humanity
no longer stands.   Men from our own country
stamp out, burn back, flush up from their refuge
with gasses, howling or silent, whatever
human or animal remains living there.

Bereft, the mothering sky
searches our faces, searches my heart.
What have I to do with these things
that now I am left destitute.
In the midst of my happiness, the worm
of man's misery coils in my heart.

Dream disclosed to me, I too am Ishmael.

STRUCTURE OF RIME XXVIII

IN MEMORIAM WALLACE STEVENS

"That God is colouring Newton doth shew"—William Blake

Erecting beyond the boundaries of all government his grand Station and Customs,   I find what I have made there a Gate, a staking out of his art in Inconsequence.   I have in mind a poetry that will frame the willingness of the heart and deliver it over to the arrest of Time, a sentence   as if there could stand some solidity   most spacial in its intent against the drifts and appearances that arise and fall away in time from the crude events of physical space.   The Mind alone holds the consequence of the erection to be true, so that Desire and Imagination usurp the place of the Invisible Throne.

It is an angel then, weeping and yet ever attending the betrayal of the Word I mean to come to in the end.   For my sake, the blood must be somewhere in time and in its own naming of place actual, and death must be   as my own awaits me   immediate to undo from its reality the physical body, all there is of the matter of me that is mine from me. The would-be dialecticians—Inquisitors of the New Dispensation in Poetry and Historians of Opprobrium, the Realists and Materialists—come forward to hold the party line against his ideality.   There are too many listeners.   There are too many voices in the one line.   They must enter the Ideal to do so, for he has changed his mind, as if the Eternal existed only momentarily and went out with him.   The Chairman of the Politbureau gets his number   and moves to isolate his heresy. The number is no longer the same.   He has gone back into the exchange of numbers.   The phone continues ringing in the pattern of the message they strive to listen   to report to the Bureau of Poetic Numbers and Approved Measures.

This is to say to the month of April and the rainbow dancer, I am with you.   I belong to the company without number.   I shall live one hundred years and then be gone.   Here and now   only I from this life can come forward to impersonate the necessity of his being here. His, the horizon.   His, the perspectives and outlines.   His, the regulation of the relevant.   I will willingly assume his numbers among my own.

The rest is all Asia, the astral miasma, the Undoing we came from,
my version of Who-He-Is-In-Reality,   the domain of colouring invading
the Responsible.

FROM DANTE ÉTUDES

EVERYTHING SPEAKS TO ME

Everything speaks to me!   In faith
my sight is sound.   I draw from out
      the resounding mountain side
the gist of majesty.   It is at once
      a presentation out of space
awakening a spiritual enormity, and still,
      the sounding of a tone
apart from any commitment to some scale.

                    The sea
comes in on rolling surfs
      of an insistent meaning,   pounds
the sands relentlessly,   demanding
      a hearing.   I overhear
tides of myself all night in it.

            And in the sounds
that lips and tongue
and tunings of the vocal chords
within the chamber of the mouth and throat
      can send upon the air,

I answer.   It is my evocation
      of the sound I'd have
return to me.   My world in speech
answers some ultimate need I know,

aroused, pours forth upon the sands
      again and again
lines written for the audience of the sea.

Then what
is "listening"?   The ear

   imitates

another listening in its

   inner labyrinth

   —sound's alembic—

   here,

the equilibrations enter in.   Here,
   the "up" and "down" we know,

so that tones are "high" and "low", and

   words have weight in my hand
   as I write.   The argument

         is in the balance,

there where the tympanum translates
   waves of the air   invisible
         into resounding   visibilities.

The shores of the continent

   eroded

listening to the sea.

OF EMPIRE

[*De Monarchia, I, II*]

Of Empire: · "a unique princedom
   extending over all persons in time"

whether it is needful
   for the well-being of the "world",
whether its true authority comes from the "people",
whether and how "God" intends it

The individual man   having his own nature and truth
    and appropriate thereto   his household
outlined   in relation to groups   he finds
    himself in   freely attending, changing,
    electing,   or joining to carry forward
        the idea, the insistent phrase,
        the needed resonance   into action,

seeks to realize harmonies in his district
(his order of life amongst the orders, savoring
    variety, seeking out his   space and time,
        his life-style)
                            a tuning
    (his appropriateness)

and in the city   develops themes
    coordinations,   names places and times,
    draws perspectives,   advances horizons,
    humanities,   public works,

and in the nation   (thus, Olson in MAXIMUS)
                to initiate
    "another kind of nation"   •

Who are the "people" when "Man" comes into it?

    For the "world" read "Earth"

and we know well enough then
    what "sin" and "well-being" are.

        Let the meaning of "nation"

be brought under the orders of the living.

THE HOUSEHOLD

The household   to provide shelter
and to prepare its members
    to live well   even

in atonality   setting free
    rearrangements of atonement,
daily new keys in dreams,
    reappearances of the "home"
    note in the melody.

Let us call each voice, his or hers,
    "He" that leads in the rehearsal,
and "She", the Matrix or Praxis
    the potentiality of Music
                rests in

—it is a choral cantata in the Men's House—

            the spring
of that river from which
        he takes his lead—
each, in this,   wife of intention,
    husband of his welfaring there,

—the women are singing with us   this hymn
                of communal counterpoints—

in the district or stanza, to
    bring each inhabitant   freely
into the action he desires there,   to sing
    into action the song,   everywhere,
leading from the houses   into the streets and courts,
            a melodious thoroughfare
    "we" direct   in company
        that there be chance encounters
            as far as our neighborhood extends

we go with what happens—

"It remains for us only
to dwell upon the mixt rimes
        in this matter almost all
to take the fullest licence

        . . . for the sweetness
        of the whole harmony"   [*De Vulgari Eloquentia*
                                                  II, XIII]

the city designd.

        He always wove into his stanza

"one line unaccompanied by a rime
    which he calld a key"

others having their resonance
    in other parts of the city

so that district by district
    in that canzone   reminds us

in the arrangement,   every
    wisht-for License conceded,

of the familiar places
        in the last lines
    most beautifully disposed

as if they fell with rhyme

    into silence.

*

Art may yet claim for itself
in the local   grand exceptions,

as the noble seeks to adventure
    more than is expected,

verging upon eqivocation
   the theme returns resolute.

For the mixture of smooth and
rough   in one texture
tragedy   the city needs

gains in brilliancy.

CIRCULATIONS OF THE SONG

AFTER JALĀL AL-DĪN RŪMĪ

*

If I do not know where He is
   He is in the very place of my not knowing.
If I do not know who He is
   He is the very person of my not knowing.

His is the Shining Forth I know not.
My heart leaps forward   past knowing.

**

Would I prune back the overgrowth of yearning?
Free today from the shadows of what has been?
   Cut away the dead Love-wood?

It is as if Christ-rood never perisht.
It is as if the God at Delphi still returnd.

Even now, new shoots are returning   toward Shrovetide,
fresh, tender.   In the fullness of summer
   they too will be rampant.
A thousand roots of feeling tamper the ground
   for this abundance,   this
         spring water.

Ten thousand leaves of this green
work in the free flow of the sun's light.

*

Do you think I do not know what the curse of
    darkness means?   the power in confusion?
Do you think I do not remember
    the tyranny of establisht religions,
the would-be annihilating cloud of lies
    and the despairing solar malevolence
that is rumord to lie back of these?
    the madness of kings?

But now, in thought of Him,   the Lord of Night
    stirs with verges of a radiance
that is in truth dark,   darkening glances of an obscurity
    Love seeks in love,   Eros-Oberon
whose Palace is Night.   Did I tell you,
    as I meant to,   He is all about me?

It is as if Night itself
    meant to cherish me.

**

The body of this thought must be a star.

This Mind is that fathomless darkness
    racing out beyond itself,   Time
        pouring beyond time,

in the cast of whose scatterd sparklings,
    seed drift of suns,
I am all water.   I reflect
    passages of what is moving as I catch it,
the shadow of the expanding depth,
the glance fugitive and sparkling
    of but one among a million promises.

*

In this world without kings

secretly in every thing   kings are preparing.
See!   a single leaf the chance light enhances
      is annointed and   *commands* my regard.
I am in the realm of this attention *subject.*

See! over there   as if hidden   an other leaf
      in obscurity   as from the depth of its darkness
comes to light   and therein   sets up
            rule over my seeing;
all the mass of foliage I see are members now
      of this courting.   I shall derive
where I am   a court   and pay court to this
            courtesy.

                    *

How happy I am in your care, my old companion of the way!
The long awaiting,   the sometimes bitter hope,
      have sweetend in these years of the faith you keep.
How completely I said "yes" when it came to me
and continue.   Each morning awakening you set free
      another day for me.   How has your face
aged over these years to keep company with mine?
ever anew as I waken endearing.   Each night
      in the exchange of touch and speech blessing,

prepared thruout for rest.   Is it not
as if He were almost here?   as if we were

            already at rest?

                    **

The rest is an Artesian well,   an underground fountain.
The level of the water is so close,
up-welling in every season,   rising thru me
the circuit Jalāl al-Dīn Rūmī
in which   at last!   I come to read you,   you
      come to be read by me.   Releasing
freshets of feeling anew I come from.

*

But if you are the lover,   how entirely you are *He*.
How entirely He is here;   He commands me.

A blazing star in the southern hemisphere
        shines in my thought in the north
and I go forth to find rumors of him.

I am like a line cast out
        into a melodic unfolding beyond itself
                a mind hovering ecstatic
above a mouth in which the heart rises
        pouring itself into liquid and fiery speech
for the sake of a rime not yet arrived
        containing again and again resonant arrivals.

Fomalhaut,   guardian splendor of the other "sky"!
in reflection my mind is crowded with splendors.

**

Are you my soul?   my love?   my redeemer?
O no!   My soul rushes forward to you!
And, in the rushing,   is entirely given me anew.

*

The veil of speech I meant to be so frail   I
        meant to be transparent that the light
        were you to read there would reveal me,
thruout waiting,   thruout about to be naked,
        thruout trembling,   has become a net
wrapping you round about in my words
        until I cannot see you.

                Now I would tear speech away.
I want you to find me out
with none of my leads in the way.
I want you to seek my being ready
        in your own way.

**

Because He was there where deep drunk I
     yet rememberd him,
because He was ever in the lure of the moment
     awaiting me,
because *His* are the eyes of my seeing you,
yours was the mouth of the wish the tongue of my speech sought
that may never actually   have been   yours
was the sweet jet from sleep's loins
     night stirrd to arousal
in the seed of the hour I came upon;
for the glorious tree of that long ago
     acknowledged need
bursts into a like-sweet abundance of leaves,
     as if from utter Being
risings of odors and savorings
     feeding full the inner song in me.

**

Have we lived together so long,   the
     confluent streams of each his own life
into one lifetime   "ours"   flowing,
     that I do not yet ever know the first
pang?   the confused joyous rush
     of coming to myself in you?
               the leap at the brink of being
left alone?   the solitary on-going
     before you?   I am ever before you,
even in the habit of our sweet marriage
     of minds.   Yet I am not
          so sure of finding you
that I have no need for this
     reassurance,
for the embrace of our two bodies,
     for the entwining of bodies,
for the kiss,   even as the first kiss,

for the memorial seal into silence the
     lips bound,

the joyous imprint and signature of our
        being together   one
                in the immortal ellipse.

                        *

For how entirely mortal is the love I bear for you.
I bring it forward into the full fragrant
        flare,   the rosy effulgence   of a perishing tree.

As in Oz or in fairyland,   the fruits of that
        arbor   are ever changing.
All the flowering specters of my   childhood and manhood
        come into and fade into   that presence,
perilous thruout,   essential thruout
        —apple, cherry, plum—deep purple
        as night and as sweet—quince and pear—
we know they are all there   all ready,
        in each ring,   each year
they belong to the tree's inner preparing.

For how entirely a door has been flung open in me
                long prepared!
How each season of the year,   a thief,
        goes in and goes out,
bearing transgressions of tastes and odors,
        traces of me lost,
imprints of thee,   stolen hours,
        stored among my secrets.

                        **

Stand by me!   you wingd and
                dark ascendant!
Attend me!   Here!   Falling!

                        *

For I am falling out into that Nature of Me
        that includes the Cosmos it believes in

as if it were the smallest thing,   an all but invisible
      seed in the cloud of these seeds scatterd,
ever emerging from belief   beyond belief.

I shall never return into my Self;
      that "Self"   passes out of Eternity,   incidental!

He too seeks you out.   He too
      dreams of coming to this fugitive morning,
of finding His "Self" in a Time so personal
      it is lost in our coming into it.

                    *

Again you have instructed me to let go,
to hold to this falling,   this
      letting myself go.
I will succumb entirely to your intention.

        Contend with me!
      you demand.   And I am surrounded by wingd
        confusions.   He
      is everywhere,   nowhere
        now where I am.

In every irreality there is Promise.
      But there
where I am not   *He*   really is.

      In Whose Presence
it is as if I had a new name.

                    **

I am falling into an emptiness of Me,
every horizon   a brink of this emptying,
walls of who-I-am   falling into me.

How enormous to come into this need!

Let us not speak then of full filling.
In the wide Universe
    emptying Itself into me, thru me,
in the myriad of lights falling,

let us speak of the little area of light
    this lamp casts.
Let us speak of what love there is.
Let us speak of how these perishing
    things
uphold me   so that

    I fall

       into *Place.*

                     *

The child I was has been left behind.
Those who first loved me have gone on without me.
Where they were   a door has been left open   upon a solitude.
In the midst of our revelry I find myself waiting.

Every day the sun returns to this place.
Time here advances toward another summer.
These fruits again darken; these new grapes
will be black and heavy hang from their bough. The heat at noon
                                        [deepens.

Sweet and pungent each moment ripens.
Every day the sun passes over this valley.
Lengthening shadows surround me.
All day I waited. I let the sun and shadow pass over me.

Here a last clearing of sunlight is left amidst shadows.
The darkest shadow falls from my pen as it writes.
In this farewell the sun pours over me
hot as noon at five o'clock.

But in Rūmī's text it is dawn. At last

he will come for me!
"He has climbed over the horizon like the sun,"   I read.
Where have you gone?
"He is extinguishing the candles of the stars."

Come quickly here where the sun is leaving me, Beloved,
for it is time to light the lovely candles again!

**

For a moment did Beauty pass over my face?
I did not have to reach for *your* beauty.
Radiant, it entirely flowd out and thru me.

Were you talking?   Were we discoursing
        upon the mercurial Hermes?

The mysteries of quick-silver and the
        alchemical gold,
the transports of Beauty,   dissolve themselves
        and are nothing,
—are resolved again,   everything—
        a wave of my own seeing you
in the rapture of this reading.

        What were you saying?
An arrow from the shining covert of your gaze
        pierced me.   Molten informations of gold
flood into my heart, arteries and veins,
        my blood,   racing thruout with this news,
pulses in a thousand chemical
        new centers of this learning.

*

How long ago I would have been your target!
every line of my young body alert to be drawn into your sight!
All of my youth was meant to be your target.

Now so late that my body

darkens   and the gossip of years
goes on loosening the tides of
my body,   now so late that
the time of waiting itself loosens
new pains in me,   I hear
the sound of the bow-string.

    Swift, swift,   how again
and again that arrow   reaches me

    and fails to reach me!

              **

How I long for the presence of your eyes,
for in your eyes gnostic revelations
    come to me,   Hermes
darkens and quickens my speech.

I will take up geometry again.
The mysteries of here and there,   above and below,
    now and then,   demand new
figures of me.   A serpent intuition
    flickers its tongue upon the air.

Mine now the quickening of that
    shifting definition I am swaying in whose

    fascination suspended   before striking

which now opens out radiant and singing petals from itself
    so that I am lost in its apparition,
distracted in this looking into the time-sway.

I am like a snake rising in the
    mirage of the sun where
everything is swaying,   to and fro,
    noon visual dancing and,
beyond my hearing,   in seeing   I over-hear
    the messengers of the sun buzzing,   wingd.

I see and am held here in my seeing   before striking
    the honeyd glow of the woodwind dance

        singing.

                    *

In each House   He has a different name.
In each   He is expected again.

And I too change,   but you in all
    these years remain
true to me so that it most seems,
            sweet constancy
        in you I have come true
and all the rest is range.

Then *He* is range.   And from this   household ours
    Heaven is range.   In the Grand Assemblage of Lives,
            the Great Assembly-House,
this Identity, this Ever-Presence,   arranged
    rank for rank,   person for person,   each from its own
sent out from what we were   to another place
    now in the constant exchange

        renderd true.

                    **

from *Ground Work II: In the Dark* [1987]

THE SENTINELS

Earth owls in ancient burrows clumpt
the dream presents.   I could return to look.
No other fragment remains.   I wanted owls
and brought them back.   The grey-brown earth-
haunted grass and bush and bushy birds
so near to death, silent as a family photograph,
still as if the sound of a rattle were missing,
the owls shifting into the stillness, thicket and hole
alive, impassive witnesses thrive there
as ever—I've but to close my eyes and go.
The rest of that field and the company
I was among in that place are lost—ghost folk,
passing among whom I was a wraith,
awake, studious, writing, the blur
marrd and almost erased,   unmarkt events.
It was night and cold and the light there
was an after-light.   I wrapt my naked body
in my comforter against that wind.   I
do not—I can not—I will not, trying,
recite the rest.   It was grey day in an absence of the sun.
It was a place without a rattling sound,
a deaf waiting room this place is close upon.
The scratching of my pen and my bending thought
move from this margin and return.   Morning shrinks.
The owls shiver down into the secrets of an earth
I began to see when I lookt into the hole I feard
and then saw others in the clump of grass.
I was dreaming and where I dreamt a light had gone out
and in that light they blind their sight and sit
sentinel upon the brooding of owl-thought, counselings
I remember ever mute and alive, hidden in all things.

IN WAKING

    the life there was   is.

That's the fact we celebrate in passing.

        The loss

is not recent but

    known in the beginning   so that

waking in the dark I grasp my skull,

    hands finding out   the feel of it,

the lines coming thru as I find myself

    speaking,   mouthing them, "We . . ."

—toes (*mes orteils*),   naming,   flexing,

    the calves of my legs (*mes mollets*)   heavy—

I am remembering.

        What it meant

it means   a round   from other lives

    for rime.

They are members of a divine company

in this world   the other world attending

    Mind   our   *speculum*

      ". . . *wake together.*"

Their sight in us   opens   morning's vistas

    our *via imaginativa*   day's eyes.

The way Life opts   we follow thru,

    I   in your company   *seeing*   name.

In the customs of speech I have long known

    —native to what speech?—

a few words from an other language

    I am seeking

come thru   you again   where

    foreign to myself   I am

reminded   yours   in every light.

*

    Whose lions in this stage   scent already

our faltering steps   and will prey

    upon the body's marches

opening gates in night's dream enclosures

    to the disclosures of a last day

following in the wake of a time that was ours,

    years in whose count we have thrived

rip from the feast in what we are

    a further wake of what we were.

And so I come to speak of pain again.

How are you this morning?   I try out

the faint ache of coming to,   then lose all,

loosening the strain in my study of you,

drawing your sleeping face   to divine

my truth and hold

from which I move   at times like this.

*

I saw the borderguard.   I saw the sleeping lion.

Wherein I saw   fused

from dream, from reading, from what I had taken

out of that painting by Rousseau direct it seemd

yet "given"   for the sight came "back" to me from an horizon

I knew by heart   I had always   known

the lion had left his pride.

In which the guardian's dream deepens

into watch,   the moon

over all restored,

and in that place takes hold

in time.

They are the members of a wake behind speech,

      song   our echoing.

And now from Rūmī

the lion of the Lord in Love

delivers himself up from his hunger.

He lays himself down in the nets of creation to find his release.

And who am I?   the man sleeping at the border asks,

that in my love dream sleep I have become

      the guardian of the lion?

IN BLOOD'S DOMAINE   **[PASSAGES]**

The Angel Syphilis in the circle of Signators   looses its hosts   to
                                      [swarm
      mounting the stem of being   to the head
                               Baudelaire,
                            [Nietszche, Swift
     are not eased into Death
                    the undoing of Mind's rule in the
                             [brain.

"Yet it is in spirit that nature is timelessly enveloped."   And, as above
                               [so below there are
     spirochete invasions that eat at the sublime envelope,   not
                           [alien, but familiars
      Life in the dis-ease radiates   invisibilities devour my star

     and Time restless crawls in center upon center   cells of lives
                               [within life conspire

Hel shines in the very word *Health*   as *Ill* in the Divine Will
[shines.

The Angel Cancer crawls across the signs of the Zodiac to
[reach its

appointed time   and   bringing down the carnal pride
[bursts into flower—
Swift, Baudelaire, Nietzsche   into the heart Eternal
[of what Poetry is

answer to the genius and science of the Abyss.   The
[first sign of this advancing power

shows in Fear that goes   clear to the bone   to gnaw at the
[marrow.

The seeress Lou Andreas-Salomé   sees long before the hour arrives—

[mais] *"Tantôt sonnera l'heure   où le divin Hasard,*

où l'auguste Vertu, ton épouse encore vierge"   —where black the
[infected blood

gushes forth from Rilke's mouth, from his nose, from his
[rectal canal

news his whole body bears as its truth   of the septic
[rose

Où le Repentir même (oh!   la dernière auberge!)

Lovely then

that Death come to carry you away from the moment of this splendor
that bursts the cells of your body   like a million larvae triumphant

comes to life in the fruit   All the spreading seeds,   the viral
[array

taking over flesh as the earth it is
                              scarlet eruptions

And the pneumatics torn in the secret workings of the Angel Tuber-
                                        [culosis
(No, I do not speak of Evils or of Agents of Death   but these
                                        [Angels
      are attendants of lives raging within life,   under these Wings
                                        [we dread

viruses, bacilli   come home to thrive in us   où tout te dira

      "Meurs, vieux lâche!   il est trop tard!"   Die, you old
                                        [coward,
                  it is too late.   I feel the ringing of tomorrow's
                                        [bell.

But what ate at Pound's immortal Mind?   for the Cantos,   for *Les
                                        [Fleurs du Mal*
                  so eat at Mind's conscience
      what malady?   what undoing-of-all-Good   workt behind
                                        [speech?

—are the matter I come from—these poisons I must know the
                              [hidden intentions of
      where "this coil of Geryon" (Djerion) said Mr Carlyle,
                              [who now becomes

      Thomas Carlyle, not the member of Congress, but
                  the genius of "Hero Worship"   his
                              [(our) congress

And if I know not my wound   it does not appear to suppurate?   In
                                        [this intercourse
      "Adolf furious from perception"   —does this thought refer
                                        [to Hitler?

Link by link I can disown no link of this chain from my
                              [conscience.

        Would you forget the furnaces of burning meat   purity
                                                        [demands?
There is no ecstasy of Beauty in which I will not remember
                                                    [Man's misery.

        Jesus, in this passage   —He is like a man coming forward in a
                                                    [hospital theater—
            cries out: I come not to heal but to tear the scab from the
                                                [wound you wanted to forget.
            May the grass no longer spread out to cover the works of man
                                                    [in the ruin of earth.

        What Angel,   what Gift of the Poem,   has brought into my
                                                        [body
            this sickness of living?   Into the very Gloria of Life's
                                                    [theme and variations
                my own counterpart of Baudelaire's terrible Ennuie?

ILLUSTRATIVE LINES

i

This pen is where the writing flows in sight
the measuring eye follows line by line,
mouth set in the mind's movement throughout at-
tentive, tentative —let the numbers fall
into the hands   one drawing the letters   one
by one   holds the count at bay,   the other
keeps the time of an inner wave in sway.

All is enfolded in a body of thought
the body occupies.   The taut brow bends over
this work in words   studious as a lover
caught up on this telling of a tale the ear
attends the wary listening of,   as if to hear
as that reader   entirely his   other
hears the ring of truth in the sound of it
the writing is mute witness to.

ii

The eye now follows mute witness to the text
the mouthing delites to analyze
and the hand directs the mind to music—

all intellect is in this fingering of time advanced
that knows no horizon of learning—
the reaches of this aptitude for exacting measure's
　　　due　　　the heart
waits upon　　　the breath flows from—

whose then the resident identity?　　　Voice
is all.　How accurately the portraitist must draw
the instrumental skull, delineate the ear, to make
a speaking likeness,　　　for sound
　　　is what　　　everywhere
　　　　　　draws near.

iii

The body at work exemplifies the work
back of whose eyes sight surfaces lives
beyond this life rush.　　　The forehead
leads forward against its dark wave.

What works in me is not mine but
ancient survivals,　how much withheld
strives unspeakable in the word to speak
the lips refuse,　eyes
close upon to face what Man is in this.

Child, not of Our Father, but of the Abyss
where He was.　In the fires of that mine
Love comes to Grief to strike a light
again,　and Dark increases to enhance
the pathos of a brief humanity time allows
　　　　　not easily.

iv

Still the face reflects a pool of thought
having nor subject nor object

resolute in tranquility   deep the eyes
gaze into the myriad nights and days
space that is time, time that is space
beyond horizon,   nor is there a center to this Mind—
it's as if all the visible were Invisible,
identical with the blue presence of the nenuphar.

v

And lust into the luster of that glow   resolves
in memory   this depth is lustral and
      melody grows in me   dim
frequencies of that water-lily head
the hands in keeping time   address
                              to illustrate
this   almost unmoving bliss in movement
         lustrum upon lustrum float
shadowy petalld fingerd five upon five
      the right hand and the left hand
in feeling   lift the mind upon the air
         passing over the water

in this   dance beyond consciousness   leading
            —an other
unheard beat its eternal governance—
      sight and sound
pass into the transports of a lingering

         scent

         illustrious.

AFTER A LONG ILLNESS

No faculty not   ill at ease
      lets us
      begin where I must

from the failure of systems   breath
      less,   heart

and lungs water-logd.

Cloggd with light chains   the kidneys'
        condition is terminal   life

the light and the heavy,   the light
        and dark.   It has always been
close upon a particular Death, un
        disclosed   what's behind

seeing, feeling, tasting, smelling   —that Cloud!

For two years
bitterness pervaded:

in the physical body   the high   blood pressure
        the accumulation of toxins, the
        break-down of ratios,

in the psyche   "stewd in its own juices"
        the eruption of hatreds,   the prayer
—I didn't have a prayer—   your care
        alone kept my love clear.

I will be there again   the ways
        must become crosst   and again
        dark passages,   dangerous straits.

My Death attended me and I knew
        I was not going to die,
nursed me thru.   Life took hold.

        What I ate   I threw up
and crawld thru as if turnd inside out.
        Every thought I had I saw
sickend me.   Secretly
        in the dark   the filters
        of my kidneys   petrified   and my Death
rearranged the date He has with me.

*

Yes, I was afraid
of not seeing you again,   of being
         taken away, not
of dying, the specter I have long
         known as my Death is the
Lord of a Passage that unites us;
         but of
         never having come to you that other
specter of my actually living is.
         Adamant.

"I have given you a cat in the dark," the voice said.
Everything changed in what has always been there
at work in the Ground: the two titles
         "Before the War",   and now, "In the Dark"
underwrite the grand design.   The magic
         has always been there,   the magnetic purr
         run over me, the feel as of cat's fur
charging the refusal to feel.   That black stone,
         now I see, has its electric familiar.

In the real I have always known myself
         in this realm where no Wind   stirs
         no Night
turns in turn to Day,   the Pool of the motionless water,
         the absolute Stillness.   In the World, death after death.
In this realm,   no last thrall of Life stirs.
         The imagination alone knows this condition.
As if this were before the War,   before
         What Is,   in the dark this state
that knows nor sleep nor waking, nor dream
         —an eternal arrest.

Index of Titles

New Directions Paperbooks—A Partial Listing

For a complete listing request free catalog from
New Directions, 80 Eighth Avenue, New York 10011　　　　　　†Bilingual

Eugenio Montale, *It Depends.*† NDP507.
Selected Poems.† NDP193.
Paul Morand, *Fancy Goods/Open All Night.* NDP567.
Vladimir Nabokov, *Nikolai Gogol.* NDP78.
Laughter in the Dark. NDP729.
The Real Life of Sebastian Knight. NDP432.
P. Neruda, *The Captain's Verses.*† NDP345.
Residence on Earth.† NDP340.
Fully Empowered. NDP792.
New Directions in Prose & Poetry (Anthology).
Available from #17 forward to #55.
Robert Nichols, *Arrival.* NDP437.
J. F. Nims, *The Six-Cornered Snowflake.* NDP700.
Charles Olson, *Selected Writings.* NDP231.
Toby Olson, *The Life of Jesus.* NDP417.
George Oppen, *Collected Poems.* NDP418.
István Örkeny, *The Flower Show/*
The Toth Family. NDP536.
Wilfred Owen, *Collected Poems.* NDP210.
José Emilio Pacheco, *Battles in the Desert.* NDP637.
Selected Poems.† NDP638.
Michael Palmer, *At Passages.* NDP803.
Nicanor Parra, *Antipoems: New & Selected.* NDP603.
Boris Pasternak, *Safe Conduct.* NDP77.
Kenneth Patchen, *Because It Is.* NDP83.
Collected Poems. NDP284.
Selected Poems. NDP160.
Ota Pavel, *How I Came to Know Fish.* NDP713.
Octavio Paz, *Collected Poems.* NDP719.
A Draft of Shadows.† NDP489.
Selected Poems. NDP574.
Sunstone.† NDP735.
A Tale of Two Gardens. NDP841.
A Tree Within.† NDP661.
Victor Pelevin, *The Yellow Arrow;* NDP845.
Omon Ra. NDP851.
Ezra Pound, *ABC of Reading.* NDP89.
The Cantos. NDP824.
Confucius. NDP285.
Confucius to Cummings. (Anth.) NDP126.
Diptych Rome-London. NDP783.
Guide to Kulchur. NDP257.
Literary Essays. NDP250.
Personae. NDP697.
Selected Cantos. NDP304.
Selected Poems. NDP66.
Caradog Prichard, *One Moonlit Night.* NDP835.
Eça de Queirós, *Ilustrious House of Ramires.* NDP785.
Raymond Queneau, *The Blue Flowers.* NDP595.
Exercises in Style. NDP513.
Mary de Rachewiltz, *Ezra Pound.* NDP405.
Raja Rao, *Kanthapura.* NDP224.
Herbert Read, *The Green Child.* NDP208.
P. Reverdy, *Selected Poems.*† NDP346.
Kenneth Rexroth, *An Autobiographical Novel.* NDP725.
Classics Revisited. NDP621.
More Classics Revisited. NDP668.
Flower Wreath Hill. NDP724.
100 Poems from the Chinese. NDP192.
100 Poems from the Japanese.† NDP147.
Selected Poems. NDP581.
Women Poets of China. NDP528.
Women Poets of Japan. NDP527.
Rainer Maria Rilke, *Poems from The Book of Hours.*
NDP408.
Possibility of Being. (Poems). NDP436.
Where Silence Reigns. (Prose). NDP464.
Arthur Rimbaud. *Illuminations.*† NDP56.
Season in Hell & Drunken Boat.† NDP97.
Jerome Rothenberg, *Khurbn.* NDP679.
Seedings & Other Poems. NDP828.
Nayantara Sahgal, *Rich Like Us.* NDP665.
Ihara Saikaku, *The Life of an Amorous Woman.*
NDP270.

St. John of the Cross, *Poems.*† NDP341.
W. Saroyan, *Fresno Stories.* NDP793.
Jean-Paul Sartre, *Nausea.* NDP82.
The Wall (Intimacy). NDP272.
P. D. Scott, *Crossing Borders.* NDP796.
Listening to the Candle. NDP747.
Delmore Schwartz, *Selected Poems.* NDP241.
In Dreams Begin Responsibilities. NDP454.
W. G. Sebald, *The Emigrants.* NDP853.
Hasan Shah, *The Dancing Girl.* NDP777.
C. H. Sisson, *Selected Poems.* NDP826.
Stevie Smith, *Collected Poems.* NDP562.
Novel on Yellow Paper. NDP778.
A Very Pleasant Evening. NDP804.
Gary Snyder, *The Back Country.* NDP249.
Turtle Island. NDP381.
Gustaf Sobin, *Breaths' Burials.* NDP781.
Muriel Spark, *The Comforters.* NDP796.
The Driver's Seat. NDP786.
The Public Image. NDP767.
Enid Starkie, *Rimbaud.* NDP254.
Stendhal, *Three Italian Chronicles.* NDP704.
Antonio Tabucchi, *Pereira Declares.* NDP848.
Nathaniel Tarn, *Lyrics . . . Bride of God.* NDP391.
Dylan Thomas, *Adventures in Skin Trade.* NDP183.
A Child's Christmas in Wales. NDP812.
Collected Poems 1934–1952. NDP316.
Collected Stories. NDP626.
Portrait of the Artist as a Young Dog. NDP51.
Quite Early One Morning. NDP90.
Under Milk Wood. NDP73.
Tian Wen: A Chinese Book of Origins. NDP624.
Uwe Timm, *Invention of Curried Sausage.*
NDP854.
Charles Tomlinson, *Selected Poems.* NDP855.
Lionel Trilling, *E. M. Forster.* NDP189.
Tu Fu, *Selected Poems.* NDP675.
N. Tucci, *The Rain Came Last.* NDP688.
Paul Valéry, *Selected Writings.*† NDP184.
Elio Vittorini, *A Vittorini Omnibus.* NDP366.
Rosmarie Waldrop, *A Key into the Language of America.*
NDP798.
Robert Penn Warren, *At Heaven's Gate.* NDP588.
Eliot Weinberger, *Outside Stories.* NDP751.
Nathanael West, *Miss Lonelyhearts & Day of the Locust.*
NDP125.
J. Wheelwright, *Collected Poems.* NDP544.
Tennessee Williams, *Baby Doll.* NDP714.
Cat on a Hot Tin Roof. NDP398.
Collected Stories. NDP784.
The Glass Menagerie. NDP218.
Hard Candy. NDP225.
A Lovely Sunday for Creve Coeur. NDP497.
The Roman Spring of Mrs. Stone. NDP770.
Something Cloudy, Something Clear. NDP829.
A Streetcar Named Desire. NDP501.
Sweet Bird of Youth. NDP409.
Twenty-Seven Wagons Full of Cotton. NDP217.
Vieux Carre. NDP482.
William Carlos Williams. *Asphodel.* NDP794.
The Autobiography. NDP223.
Collected Poems: Vol. I. NDP730.
Collected Poems: Vol. II. NDP731.
The Collected Stories. NDP817.
The Doctor Stories. NDP585.
Imaginations. NDP329.
In The American Grain. NDP53.
Paterson. Complete. NDP806.
Pictures from Brueghel. NDP118.
Selected Poems (new ed.). NDP602.
Wisdom Books:
St. Francis. NDP477; *Taoists.* NDP509;
Wisdom of the Desert. NDP295.
Yūko Tsushima, *The Shooting Gallery.* NDP486.

For a complete listing request free catalog from
New Directions, 80 Eighth Avenue, New York 10011   †Bilingual